KNITTED
Jackets

20 Designs from Classic to Contemporary

Cheryl Oberle

INTERWEAVE.
interweavebooks.com

EDITOR Judith Durant
TECHNICAL EDITOR Lori Gayle
Cover & Interior Design Mark Lewis
Photography Joe Coca
Styling Ann Swanson
Production Design Katherine Jackson

 Interweave Press LLC
201 East Fourth Street
Loveland, CO 80537-5655 USA
interweavebooks.com

Printed in China through Asia Pacific Offset

Library of Congress
Cataloging-in-Publication Data

Oberle, Cheryl, 1955-
  Knitted jackets : 20 designs from
classic to contemporary / Cheryl Oberle,
author.
      p. cm.
  Includes index.
  ISBN 978-1-59668-026-5 (pbk.)
  1. Knitting--Patterns. 2. Jackets. I. Title.
  TT825.O244 2008
  746.43'2041--dc22

              2008014307

10 9 8 7 6 5 4 3 2 1

To all who knit beauty into the world,
and to
Gary Andrew Oberle
this book is gratefully and lovingly dedicated.

Contents

Introduction   4

I Simplicity   6
Box Top   8
Tyrolean Jacket   14
Three Sisters   20
Seedling   26
Rachel's Jacket   32
Cusco   36
The Wrapper   40

II Contrast   44
Northwest Celtic   46
Dakota on the Side   54
Baltic Bodice   60
Wabi Sabi   64
Bergen   70

III Texture   78
Bloomsbury Jacket   80
Puzzle Me This   88
Edwardian Day Coat   96
Edo   104
Little Edo   110
Ivory Leaves   114
Scholar's Jacket   120
Inish   128

IV Materials & Techniques 134
Acknowledgments   142
Resources   143
Bibliography   143
Index   144

Knitting on the Outside

The creation of something new is not accomplished by the intellect but by the play of instinct acting from inner necessity. The creative mind plays with the objects it loves.

—Carl Jung

"Put on your jacket!"
For centuries this sage advice has been heeded in cultures around the world. Jackets are worn for warmth, for work, and for style. A jacket is often the outermost layer of our appearance to the world and so it is indeed a special thing. A jacket can identify one as part of a society or distinguish one as an individualist.

My working title for this book was "Knitting on the Outside" for not only are jackets the garments that we wear "outside," but also these jackets themselves are slightly "outside" in terms of their design. While largely influenced by cultures from around the world, these are jackets of inspiration rather than of replication.

Knitted jackets vary widely in style from short and fitted to long and roomy. Structure of the jackets is, for the most part, simple; there is no elaborate shaping and most are designed to have a minimum number of seams, allowing them to be "knitted together" rather than sewn. Jackets, which by definition fit over the top of other garments, need to have a bit of extra ease to do so. The finished sizes and fit description in each pattern, along with the standard size chart in Materials and Techniques, will guide you in choosing a size. Sleeve length is the most variable among individuals, so for most of these designs, making a sleeve longer or shorter at the cuff is the simplest and most elegant solution. Blocking your jacket will give it its final dimensions and a professional finish. Blocking is what makes a knitted jacket shine. Detailed directions for blocking are also in Materials and Techniques.

I have used many of my favorite yarns for *Knitted Jackets*, and each pattern has detailed yarn information. Each yarn description is accompanied by the Craft Yarn Council's standard weight symbol, and the Materials and Techniques chapter supplies guidelines to make yarn substitution easy.

Special knitting techniques used in each jacket are listed in the patterns and are described in the Materials and Techniques section, where you'll also find a key to the abbreviations used in the patterns. While this book is not intended to teach you to knit, I hope that there are tools here that you will take with you into your knitting life.

As it was with my earlier books, *Folk Shawls* and *Folk Vests,* the creation of *Knitted Jackets* has been a great journey. My dearest hope is that *Knitted Jackets* will be for you, the knitter, what it has been for me—a celebration of knitting!

Simplicity is the ultimate sophistication.

—*Leonardo da Vinci*

Simplicity

Simple shapes and simple stitches
are well suited to everyday jackets.
The jackets in this section showcase
special yarns beautifully with their
straightforward knitting and
interesting construction details.

During the 1950s, while kids collected cereal box tops to mail away for prizes, women were embracing boxy, easy fitting jackets in highly textured wools. This version has not only the correct boxy shape but also uses an easy box stitch pattern.

Box Top

"A box without hinges, key, or lid, yet golden treasure inside is hid."

—J. R. R. Tolkein

FINISHED SIZE
47½ (51, 54½)" (120.5 [129.5, 138.5] cm) chest circumference. Jacket shown measures 51" (129.5 cm). Box Top is oversize (see fit guidelines on page 136).

YARN (4)
Shown here: Schoolhouse Press Sheepsdown (100% wool; 85 yd [78 m]/4 oz [113 g]): Pale Gray, 9 (10, 11) skeins.

NEEDLES
Size 11 (8 mm): 24" (60-cm) and 16" (40-cm) circular needles (cir).
Adjust needle size if necessary to obtain the correct gauge.

NOTIONS
Markers (m); safety pin (optional); smooth cotton scrap yarn for holders; crochet hook size H/8 (5 mm); three 1½" (3.8 cm) buttons.

GAUGE
9 stitches and 16 rows/rounds = 4" (10 cm) in Box Stitch patterns.

Techniques

Three-needle bind-off (page 138), pick up by knitting (page 137); crochet slip stitch (page 136), crochet chain stitch (page 136).

Stitch Guide

Box Stitch Worked Flat
(multiple of 4 sts plus 2)

Row 1: (RS) K2,*p2, k2; rep from *.
Row 2: P2,*k2, p2; rep from *.
Row 3: Rep Row 2.
Row 4: Rep Row 1.
Rep Rows 1–4 for patt.

Box Stitch Worked Circularly
(multiple of 4 sts, plus 2)

Rnds 1 and 2: K2,*p2, k2; rep from *.
Rnds 3 and 4: P2, *k2, p2; rep from *.
Rep Rnds 1–4 for patt. Note: Each rnd deliberately begins and ends with the same 2 sts (i.e., either k2 or p2).

Notes

» The lower body is worked in one piece to the armholes, then the back and fronts are divided and worked separately to the shoulders.

» Place a safety pin on the RS of the fabric to distinguish it from the WS.

LOWER BODY

With longer cir, CO 106 (114, 122) sts. Beg Box St Worked Flat (see Stitch Guide), placing markers (pm) in Row 1 as foll: (RS) Work 28 (30, 32) sts in patt for right front, pm for right side, work 50 (54, 58) sts in patt for back, pm for left side, work 28 (30, 32) sts in patt for left front. Continue even in patt until piece measures 15½ (16, 16½" (39.5 [40.5, 42] cm) from CO, ending with a RS row.

Reserve Underarms and Fronts

Next row: (WS, Row 2 or 4 of patt) Work in patt to 4 sts past the first marker (m), place the last 8 sts worked on holder for left armhole, leaving m in place to identify the center of these sts later, work in patt to 4 sts past the second m, place the last 8 sts worked (including m) on holder for right armhole, work in patt to end for right front—24 (26, 28) sts each for right and left fronts; 42 (46, 50) sts for back. Break yarn. Place both fronts on holders.

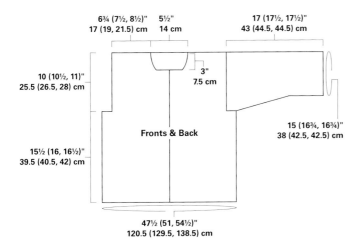

6¾ (7½, 8½)"   5½"
17 (19, 21.5) cm   14 cm

17 (17½, 17½)"
43 (44.5, 44.5) cm

10 (10½, 11)"
25.5 (26.5, 28) cm

3"
7.5 cm

Fronts & Back

15 (16¾, 16¾)"
38 (42.5, 42.5) cm

15½ (16, 16½)"
39.5 (40.5, 42) cm

47½ (51, 54½)"
120.5 (129.5, 138.5) cm

BACK

Rejoin yarn to 42 (46, 50) back sts on needle with RS
facing. Continue in established patt until piece measures
10 (10½, 11" (25.5 [26.5, 28] cm) above underarm, ending
with a WS row. Place sts on holder.

RIGHT FRONT

Place 24 (26, 28) right front sts on longer cir and rejoin
yarn with RS facing at neck edge. Continue in established
patt until piece measures 7 (7½, 8)" (18 [19, 20.5] cm)
above underarm, ending with a WS row.

Shape Neck

Next row: (RS) Work 6 sts in patt and place these 6 sts
on holder for the front neck, work in patt to end—18 (20,
22) sts. Turn, and work 1 WS row. **Dec row:** (RS) K1, ssk,
work in patt to end of row—1 st dec'd. Rep the dec row
every RS row 2 more times—15 (17, 19) sts rem. Work
even until piece measures 10 (10½, 11)" (25.5 [26.5, 28]
cm) above underarm, ending with same WS patt row as for
back. Place sts on holder.

LEFT FRONT

Place 24 (26, 28) left front sts on longer cir and rejoin yarn with RS facing at armhole edge. Continue in established patt until piece measures 7 (7½, 8)" (18 [19, 20.5] cm) above underarm, ending with a WS row.

Shape Neck

Next row: (RS) Work in patt to end of row, break yarn, and place last 6 sts worked on holder for the front neck—18 (20, 22) sts. Turn, rejoin yarn with WS facing, and work 1 WS row. **Dec row:** (RS) Work in patt to last 3 sts, k2tog, k1—1 st dec'd. Rep the dec row every RS row 2 more times—15 (17, 19) sts rem. Work even until piece measures same as left front above underarm, ending with same WS patt row as for back and right front. Place sts on holder.

JOIN SHOULDERS

With WS of pieces touching and RS facing outwards, join 15 (17, 19) front and back shoulder sts using the three-needle bind-off method—12 sts rem on holder for center back neck for all sizes. The bind-off ridge will form a decorative welt on the outside of the garment.

SLEEVES

Note: Stitches for the sleeves are picked up around the armhole and the sleeves are worked circularly down to the wrist. With shorter cir and beg at m in center of held underarm sts, k4 from holder, pick up by knitting 21 (23, 25) sts along armhole edge to shoulder join, then 21 (23, 25) sts along armhole edge to underarm, k4 rem held underarm sts—50 (54, 58) sts. Join for working in the rnd, and pm for beg of rnd. Work in Box St Worked Circularly (see Stitch Guide) for 6 (8, 8) rnds.

Sleeve Shaping

Dec rnd: K2tog, work in established patt to last 2 sts, ssk—2 sts dec'd. Rep the dec rnd every 4th rnd 7 (7, 9) more times—34 (38, 38) sts. Work even in patt until sleeve measures 17 (17½, 17½)" (43 [44.5, 44.5] cm) from pick-up rnd. BO in patt.

FINISHING

Collar (same for all sizes)

With RS facing and longer cir, work 6 sts from right front neck holder in established patt, pick up by knitting 10 sts along right neck to shoulder join, pick up 1 st in shoulder, work 12 back neck sts in established patt, pick up 1 st in shoulder join, pick up by knitting 10 sts along left front neck, work 6 sts from left front neck holder in established patt—46 sts. Work even in established patt for 13 rows, beg and ending with a WS row. BO in patt.

Button loops

Make 3 button loops on right front as foll: With RS facing and using crochet hook, join yarn to right front edge 4" (10 cm) down from bound-off edge of collar. Working from RS, work 1 slip stitch in front edge, work 5 crochet chain sts, work 1 slip stitch in front edge 7 rows below starting slip stitch, fasten off last st and break yarn. Work 2 more loops in the same manner, starting rem loops 10" (25.5 cm) and 16" (40.5 cm) down from bound-off edge of collar.

Sew buttons into place on left front to correspond to button loops.

In the region of the Austrian Alps known as the Tyrol, mountaineering is considered both a physical and spiritual pursuit. The intense concentration necessary to climb a peak is known as the "meditation on the mountain." This jacket is based on the traditional climber's jacket.

Tyrolean Jacket

"Anyone who keeps the ability to see beauty never grows old."

—Austrian Proverb

FINISHED SIZE
38 (42, 46)" (96.5 [106.5, 117] cm) chest circumference. Jacket shown measures 42" (106.5 cm). Tyrolean is standard fitting (see fit guidelines on page 136).

YARN 2
Shown here: Jamieson and Smith 2 Ply Jumper Weight (100% wool, about 130 yd [119 m]/25 g): #FC44 Acorn (A), 14 (15, 17) balls; #0077 Black (B), 3 balls for all sizes.

NEEDLES
Size 4 (3.5 mm): 24" (60-cm) circular needle (cir).
Adjust needle size if necessary to obtain the correct gauge.

NOTIONS
Safety pin; markers (m); smooth cotton scrap yarn for holders; six ½" (1.3 cm) lightweight buttons.

GAUGE
24 stitches and 56 rows = 4" (10 cm) in garter stitch.

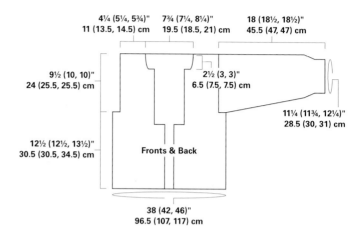

4¼ (5¼, 5¾)"
11 (13.5, 14.5) cm

7¾ (7¼, 8¼)"
19.5 (18.5, 21) cm

18 (18½, 18½)"
45.5 (47, 47) cm

9½ (10, 10)"
24 (25.5, 25.5) cm

2½ (3, 3)"
6.5 (7.5, 7.5) cm

11¼ (11¾, 12¼)"
28.5 (30, 31) cm

12½ (12½, 13½)"
30.5 (30.5, 34.5) cm

Fronts & Back

38 (42, 46)"
96.5 (107, 117) cm

LOWER BODY

With A, CO 216 (242, 264) sts. Place markers (m) as foll: (RS) K52 (59, 63), place marker (pm) for right side, k112 (124, 138) for back, pm for left side, k52 (59, 63) to end for left front. Work in garter st (knit all sts every row) until piece measures 10½ (10½, 11½)" (26.5 [26.5, 29] cm) from CO, ending with a WS row.

Reserve Front Insets and Underarms

BO 11 sts beg of next 2 rows for front insets—194 (220, 242) sts rem. Cont in garter st for 2" (5 cm) more, ending with a RS row—piece measures about 12½ (12½, 13½)" (31.5 [31.5, 34.5] cm) from CO. Next row: (WS) Knit to 7 (8, 9) sts past the first m, place the last 14 (16, 18) sts worked on holder for left armhole, leaving m in place to identify the center of these sts later, knit to 7 (8, 9) sts past the second m, place the last 14 (16, 18) sts worked (including m) on holder for right armhole, knit to end of row—34 (40, 43) sts each for right and left fronts; 98 (108, 120) sts for back. Break yarn. Place both fronts on holders.

Back

Rejoin A to 98 (108, 120) back sts on needle with RS facing. Beg with a RS row, work in garter st until back measures 9½ (10, 10)" (24 [25.5, 25.5] cm) from underarm, ending with a RS row. Place back sts on holder.

Right Front

Place 34 (40, 43) held right front sts on needle and rejoin A with RS facing. Beg with a RS row, work in garter st until piece measures 7" (18 cm) above underarm for all sizes, ending with a WS row.

Shape Neck

Next row: (RS) K5 and place these sts on holder for front neck, knit to end—29 (35, 38) sts. Turn work and knit 1 WS row. **Dec row:** (RS) K1, ssk, work to end of row—1 st dec'd at neck edge. Rep the dec row every RS row 2 more times—26 (32, 35) sts rem. Work even until front measures 9½ (10, 10)" (24 [25.5, 25.5] cm) from underarm, ending with a RS row. Place sts on holder.

Left Front

Place 34 (40, 43) held left front sts on needle and rejoin A with RS facing. Beg with a RS row, work in garter st until piece measures 7" (18 cm) above underarm for all sizes, ending with a WS row.

Shape Neck

Next row: (RS) Knit to end of row, place last 5 sts worked on holder for front neck, break yarn—29 (35, 38) sts. Turn work, rejoin A with WS facing, and knit 1 WS row. **Dec row:** (RS) Knit to last 3 sts, k2tog, k1—1 st dec'd at neck edge. Rep the dec row every RS row 2 more times—26 (32, 35) sts rem. Work even until front measures 9½ (10, 10)" (24 [25.5, 25.5] cm) from underarm, ending with a RS row. Place sts on holder.

JOIN SHOULDERS

With WS of pieces touching and RS facing outward, join 26 (32, 35) front and back shoulder sts using the three-needle bind-off method—46 (44, 50) sts rem on holder for center back neck. The bind-off ridge will form a decorative welt on the outside of the garment.

SLEEVES

Notes: Because there can be a significant difference in gauge between garter stitch worked circularly and garter stitch worked flat, the sleeve stitches are picked up around the armhole and knitted back and forth in rows to the wrist. A "seam" stitch is created by slipping the first stitch of every row to make seaming easier, and the decreases are worked inside these slipped edge stitches. Beg at marker of held underarm sts, k7 (8, 9) sts from holder, pick up and knit 49 (51, 52) sts along armhole edge to shoulder join (about 3 sts for every 4 garter ridges, i.e., pick up 1 st from 3 ridges in a row, then skip 1 ridge), pick up by knitting 49 (51, 52) sts along armhole edge to underarm, k7 (8, 9) rem held underarm sts—112 (118, 122) sts. Knit 7 (11, 11) rows, slipping the first st of each row pwise wyf, bring yarn to back, then knit to end of row. Slip the first st of every non-shaping row in the same manner hereafter.

Sleeve Shaping

Dec row: (RS) Sl 1, k2tog, knit to last 3 sts, ssk, k1—2 sts dec'd. Rep the dec row every 12th row 14 (15, 16) more times—82 (86, 88) sts rem. Work even until sleeve measures 14½ (14¾, 14¾)" (37 [37.5, 37.5] cm) from pick-up row, ending with a WS row.

Cuff

Change to color B, and knit 2 rows even. **Next row:** (RS) Knit, dec 5 sts evenly spaced—77 (81, 83) sts. Rep the 5-st dec row every 10th (12th, 12th) row 2 more times—67 (71, 73) sts. Work even until cuff measures 3½ (3¾, 3¾)" (9 [9.5, 9.5] cm) from beg of color B, ending with a RS row—sleeve measures about 18 (18½, 18½)" (45.5 [47, 47] cm) from pick-up row. BO all sts on WS. Sew sleeve seam using matching colors for each section.

FINISHING

Right Front Inset

With RS facing and color B, beg at lower corner of right front inset, pick up by knitting 46 sts along right front edge as for sleeves. Work in garter st for 23 rows, ending with a WS row. Place sts on holder. Sew inset selvedge to bound-off sts of lower body.

Right Front Band

With RS facing and color B, beg at lower edge of right front, pick up by knitting 56 (56, 60) sts along right front edge as for sleeves, knit 46 inset sts from holder—102 (102, 106) sts. Work in garter st for 10 (10, 12) rows, slipping the first st every RS row pwise wyf, and ending with a RS row. BO all sts loosely.

Left Front Inset

With RS facing and color B, beg at neck edge of left front inset, pick up by knitting 46 sts along left front edge. Work in garter st for 23 rows, ending with a WS row. Place sts on holder. Sew inset selvedge to bound-off sts of lower body.

Left Front Band

With RS facing and color B, beg at neck edge of left front inset, knit 46 inset sts from holder, then pick up and knit 56 (56, 60) sts along left front to lower edge—102 (102, 106) sts. Work in garter st for 10 (10, 12) rows, slipping the first st every RS row pwise wyf, and ending with a RS row. BO all sts loosely.

Collar

With RS facing and color B, beg at bound-off edge of right front inset and picking up by knitting as for sleeves, pick up 15 sts along selvedge of inset, knit 5 sts from neck holder, pick up 14 (18, 18) sts along right neck to shoulder join, knit 46 (44, 50) back neck sts from holder, pick up 14 (18, 18) sts along left front neck to holder, knit 5 sts from holder, pick up 15 sts along selvedge of left front inset—114 (120, 126) sts. Knit 13 rows, slipping the first st of every row pwise wyf, and ending with a WS row. **Collar dec row:** (RS) Slip first st of row pwise wyf, ssk, work to last 3 sts, k2tog, k1—2 sts dec'd. Rep collar dec row on next 2 RS rows—108 (114, 120) sts. BO all sts loosely.

Sew 3 buttons to each front inset as shown in photograph at left.

The Three Sisters is named for the three basic stitch "sisters" used in the design; the body is *stockinette* stitch with one *cable* panel and *garter* stitch borders. The combination of technique and ease of knitting makes Three Sisters a good choice for both new knitters with advancing skills and for experienced knitters in search of classic style.

"Sisters are different flowers from the same garden."

—Anonymous

Three Sisters

FINISHED SIZE
42 (47, 53)" (106.5 [119.5, 134.5] cm) chest circumference. Jacket shown measures 47" (119.5 cm). Three Sisters is loose fitting (see fit guidelines on page 136).

YARN (4)
Shown here: Cheryl Oberle's Reflections Hand-dyed (55% mohair, 45% merino; about 325 yd [297m]/8 oz [227 g]): Moss, 4 (4, 5) hanks.

NEEDLES
Body and sleeves—size 9 (5.5 mm) 24" and 16" (60- and 40-cm) circular (cir), and set of 4 double-pointed (dpn). Bottom border and cuffs—size 6 (4 mm) 24" (60-cm) cir and set of 4 dpn. Front and neck border—size 7 (4.5 mm) 24" (60-cm) cir.
Adjust needle size if necessary to obtain the correct gauge.

NOTIONS
Markers (m); smooth cotton scrap yarn for holders; cable needle (cn); crochet hook size G/7 or H/8 (4.5 or 5 mm) optional; one 1½" (3.8 cm) button (optional).

GAUGE
16 stitches and 24 rows = 4" (10 cm) in stockinette using largest needles; 20-st cable panel from chart measures about 3¼" (8.5 cm) wide using largest needles.

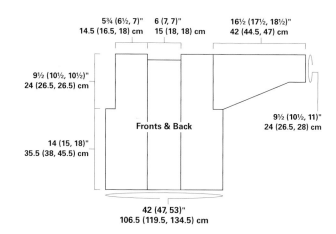

Techniques

K1f&b increase (page 137), chart reading (see page 139), three-needle bind-off (page 138), pick up by knitting (page 137), crochet chain stitch (optional, page 136).

Note

» The lower body is worked in one piece to the armholes, then the back and fronts are divided and worked separately to the shoulders.

Diagram labels:
- 5¾ (6½, 7)" / 14.5 (16.5, 18) cm
- 6 (7, 7)" / 15 (18, 18) cm
- 16½ (17½, 18½)" / 42 (44.5, 47) cm
- 9½ (10½, 10½)" / 24 (26.5, 26.5) cm
- 9½ (10½, 11)" / 24 (26.5, 28) cm
- Fronts & Back
- 14 (15, 18)" / 35.5 (38, 45.5) cm
- 42 (47, 53)" / 106.5 (119.5, 134.5) cm

LOWER BODY

Bottom Border

With smallest 24" (60-cm) cir, CO 147 (163, 187) sts. Work in garter st (knit all sts every row) for 10 (10, 12) rows, ending with a WS row—piece measures about 1½ (1½, 1¾)" (3.8 [3.8, 4.5] cm) from CO.

Body

Change to largest 24" (60-cm) cir. Next row: (RS) K3, place marker (pm) for beg of cable panel, p2, k1f&b, k2, k1f&b, p2, k1f&b, k2, k1f&b, p4, pm for end of cable panel, k14 (17, 23), pm for right side, k84 (94, 106) for back, pm for left side, k30 (33, 39) for left front—151 (167, 191) sts total: 37 (40, 46) right front sts with 20 sts between m for cable panel; 30 (33, 39) left front sts; 84 (94, 106) back sts. **Note:** Throughout the rest of the body, work all sts except the marked cable panel in St st. Next row: (WS) Purl to first cable panel m, work Set-up Row of Cable chart over next 20 sts, purl to end of row. Continue in St st outside cable panel m, and rep only Rows 1–32

of chart in marked cable section (do not rep Set-up Row) until piece measures 14 (15, 18)" (35.5 [38, 45.5] cm) from CO, ending with a RS row.

Reserve Underarms and Fronts

Next row: (WS) Work in patt to 7 (7, 11) sts past the first side m, place the last 14 (14, 22) sts worked on holder for left armhole, leaving m in place to identify the center of these sts later, work in patt to 7 (7, 11) sts past the next side m, place the last 14 (14, 22) sts worked (including m) on a holder for right armhole, work in patt to end of right front—30 (33, 35) sts for right front; 23 (26, 28) sts for left front; 70 (80, 84) sts for back. Break yarn. Place both fronts on holders.

BACK

Rejoin yarn to 70 (80, 84) back sts on needle with RS facing. Continue in St st until back measures 8½ (9½, 9½)" (21.5 [24, 24] cm) from the underarm, ending with a RS row.

Cable

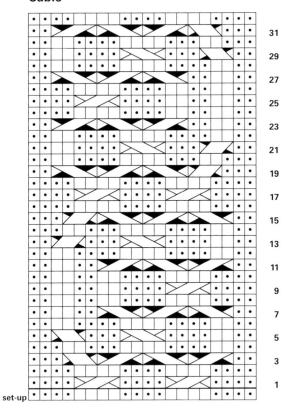

□	k on RS; p on WS
·	p on RS; k on WS
⟋	sl 1 st onto cn and hold in back, k2, p1 from cn
⟍	sl 2 sts onto cn and hold in front, p1, k2 from cn
⟍	sl 2 sts onto cn and hold in back, k2, k2 from cn
⟋	sl 2 sts onto cn and hold in front, k2, k2 from cn
◢	sl 2 sts onto cn and hold in back, k2, p2 from cn
◣	sl 2 sts onto cn and hold in front, p2, k2 from cn

Back Neck and Shoulder Shaping

Next row: (WS) P23 (26, 28) for left shoulder, place rem 47 (54, 56) sts on holder. Work even in St st on left shoulder sts for 5 more rows, beg and ending with a RS row—piece measures about 9½ (10½, 10½)" (24 [26.5, 26.5] cm) above underarm. Place left shoulder sts on holder. Place 23 (26, 28) sts for right shoulder on largest cir, leaving center 24 (28, 28) sts on holder for back neck. Rejoin yarn to right shoulder sts with WS facing. Beg with WS row, work even in St st for 6 rows, ending with a RS row—piece measures same as left shoulder above underarm. Place right shoulder sts on holder.

LEFT FRONT

Place 23 (26, 28) held left front sts on largest cir and rejoin yarn with RS facing at armhole edge. Work in St st until piece measures 9½ (10½, 10½)" (24 [26.5, 26.5] cm) above underarm, ending with a WS row. Place sts on holder.

RIGHT FRONT

Place 30 (33, 35) held right front sts on largest cir and rejoin yarn with RS facing at neck edge. Work in established patts until piece measures 9½ (10½, 10½)" (24 [26.5, 26.5] cm) above underarm, ending with a WS row, and dec 7 sts evenly spaced in last row—23 (26, 28) sts. Place sts on holder.

JOIN SHOULDERS

With WS of pieces touching and RS facing outward, join 23 (26, 28) front and back shoulder sts using the three-needle bind-off method—24 (28, 28) sts rem on holder for back neck. The bind-off ridge will form a decorative welt on the outside of the garment.

SLEEVES

Note: Stitches for the sleeves are picked up around the armhole and the sleeves are worked circularly down to the wrist. With 16" (40-cm) cir in largest size and beg at m in center of held underarm sts, k7 (7, 11) from holder, pick up by knitting 38 (42, 41) sts along armhole edge to shoulder join, then 38 (42, 41) sts along armhole edge to underarm, k7 (7, 11) rem underarm sts—90 (98, 104) sts. Join for working in the rnd, and pm for beg of rnd. Purl 1 rnd, then knit 5 rnds.

Sleeve Shaping

Dec rnd: K1, k2tog, knit to last 2 sts, ssk—2 sts dec'd. Rep the dec rnd every 3rd rnd 25 (27, 29) more times, changing to larger dpn when there are too few sts to fit comfortably around the cir—38 (42, 44) sts; piece measures about 13¾ (14¾, 15¾)" (35 [37.5, 40] cm) from pick-up rnd. Work even in St st until piece measures 14½ (15½, 16½)" (37 [39.5, 42] cm) from pick-up rnd, or 2" (5 cm) less than desired length.

Cuff

Change to smaller dpn. Beg with a purl round, work circularly in garter st (purl 1 rnd, knit 1 rnd) for 16 rnds—piece measures about 16½ (17½, 18½)" (42 [44.5, 47] cm) from pick-up rnd. BO loosely as if to purl.

FINISHING
Front and Neck Border

With middle-size 24" (60-cm) cir and RS facing, beg at lower edge of right front pick up by knitting 89 (97, 107) sts along right front to shoulder join, 3 sts along side of back neck to holder, k24 (28, 28) sts from back neck holder, pick up by knitting 3 sts along other side of back neck, then 89 (97, 107) sts along left front from shoulder join lower edge—208 (228, 248) sts. Work even in garter st for 26 (28, 28) rows, ending with a RS row—piece measures about 3 (3¼, 3¼)" (7.5 [8.5, 8.5] cm) from pick-up row. BO loosely as if to knit. **Tip:** BO using a larger needle to keep bind-off loose and flexible.

Button Loop and Button (*optional*)

Leaving a long tail at each end, use crochet hook to work a crochet chain about 2½" (6.5 cm) long. Use tails to attach chain to WS of right front border, one garter ridge in from bound-off edge and about 4½ (5, 6)" (11.5 [12.5, 15] cm) up from CO edge. Sew button in position on left front, just to the right of the front border pick-up row as shown in photograph on page 20.

The close-fitting cropped jacket is found in cultures around the world. From Scandinavia to Morocco and from Bali to New York, this shape is worn whenever just an extra touch of warmth or style is needed for the upper body. Seedling pays homage to this useful and charming style of jacket. Give it a try—you might find more than one "cropping up" in your knitting basket.

Seedling

"Dreams are the seedlings of realities."

—James Allen, New Zealand Statesman

FINISHED SIZE
36 (40, 44)" (91.5 [101.5, 112] cm) chest circumference. Jacket shown measures 40" (101.5 cm). Seedling is close fitting (see fit guidelines on page 136).

YARN (4)
Shown here: La Lana Wools of Taos Forever Random Fines Obverse (60% Romney wool, 40% yearling mohair; about 118 yd [108 m]/2 oz [57 g]): Zulu Prince, 7 (8, 8) skeins

NEEDLES
Body—sizes 7 and 9 (4.5 mm and 5.5 mm): 24" (60-cm) circular needles (cir). Sleeves—size 9 (5.5 mm): 16" (40-cm) cir, and set of 4 double-pointed (dpn) and size 8 (5 mm): set of 4 double-pointed (dpn).
Adjust needle size if necessary to obtain the correct gauge.

NOTIONS
Safety pin; markers (m); smooth cotton scrap yarn for holders; four ⁵/₈" (1.6 cm) buttons.

GAUGE
14 stitches and 24 rows = 4" (10 cm) in seed stitch using larger needles.

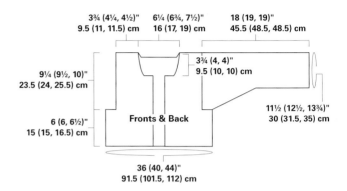

LOWER BODY

Bottom Border

With smaller 24" (60-cm) cir, CO 118 (130, 144) sts. Place markers (pm) as foll: (RS) Work 29 (32, 35) sts in seed st, pm for right side, work 60 (66, 74) sts in established seed st for back, pm for left side, work 29 (32, 35) sts in established seed st to end. Work 3 more rows in seed st, ending with a WS row.

Body

Change to larger 24" (60-cm) cir, and continue in patt as established until piece measures 6 (6, 6½)" (15 [15, 16.5] cm) from CO edge, ending with a RS row.

Reserve Underarms and Fronts

Next row: (WS) Work in patt as established to 6 (6, 8) sts past the first m, place the last 12 (12, 16) sts worked on holder for left armhole, leaving m in place to identify the center of these sts later, work to 6 (6, 8) sts past the second m, place the last 12 (12, 16) sts worked (including m) on a holder for right armhole, work to end of row—23 (26, 27) sts each for right and left fronts; 48 (54, 58) sts for back. Break yarn. Place both fronts on holders.

BACK

Rejoin yarn to 48 (54, 58) back sts on needle with RS facing. Beg with a RS row, continue in patt as established until back measures 8½ (8¾, 9¼)" (21.5 [22, 23.5] cm) from the underarm, ending with a RS row.

Reserve Neck Stitches

Next row: (WS) Work 15 (17, 18) sts in pattern for the left shoulder, place center 18 (20, 22) sts on a holder for back neck, then place rem 15 (17, 18) sts on a separate holder for the right shoulder—15 (17, 18) sts rem on needle for the left shoulder.

Left Shoulder and Neck Shaping

Continue in patt as follows on sts of left shoulder only:

Row 1: (RS) K1, ssk, work in patt to end of row—
   1 st dec'd at neck edge.

Row 2: Work even in patt as established.

Rep Rows 1 and 2 once more—13 (15, 16) sts rem; piece measures 9¼ (9½, 10)" (23.5 [24, 25.5] cm) above underarm. Place sts on holder.

Right Shoulder and Neck Shaping

Place 15 (17, 18) held right shoulder sts on needle and rejoin yarn with WS facing. Beg with a WS row at neck edge, work 1 row even in patt as established.

Row 1: (RS) Work in patt to last 3 sts, k2tog, k1—1 st dec'd at neck edge.

Row 2: Work even in patt as established.

Rep Rows 1 and 2 once more—13 (15, 16) sts rem; right shoulder measures same as left shoulder above underarm. Place sts on holder.

LEFT FRONT

Place 23 (26, 27) held left front sts on needle and rejoin yarn with RS facing at armhole edge. Beg with a RS row and keeping patt as established, work in seed st until the front measures 5½ (5½, 6)" (14 [14, 15] cm) above under-arm, ending with a RS row. Break yarn.

Shape Neck

Next row: (WS) Place first 7 (8, 8) sts on a holder, rejoin yarn to next st, and work in pattern as established to end of row—16 (18, 19) sts. Continue neck shaping as follows:

Row 1: (RS) Work in patt to last 3 sts, k2tog, k1—
1 st dec'd at neck edge.

Row 2: Work even in patt as established.

Rep Rows 1 and 2 two more times—13 (15, 16) sts rem. Work even in patt until left front measures 9¼ (9½, 10)" (23.5 [24, 25.5] cm) above underarm. Place sts on holder.

RIGHT FRONT

Place 23 (26, 27) held right front sts on needle and rejoin yarn with RS facing at center front edge. Beg with a RS row and keeping patt as established, work in seed st until the front measures 5½ (5½, 6)" (14 [14, 15] cm) above underarm, ending with a RS row.

Shape Neck

Next row: (WS) Work in patt as established to the last 7 (8, 8) sts, and place these sts on holder—16 (18, 19) sts. Continue neck shaping as follows:

Row 1: (RS) K1, ssk, work in patt to end of row—
1 st dec'd at neck edge.

Row 2: Work even in patt as established.

Rep Rows 1 and 2 two more times—13 (15, 16) sts rem. Work even in patt until right front measures 9¼ (9½, 10)" (23.5 [24, 25.5] cm) above underarm. Place sts on holder.

JOIN SHOULDERS

With RS of pieces touching and WS facing outward, join 13 (15, 16) front and back shoulder sts using the three-needle bind-off method.

SLEEVES

Note: Stitches for the sleeves are picked up around the armhole and the sleeves are worked circularly down to the wrist. Using 16" (40-cm) cir, beg at marker in center of held underarm sts k6 (6, 8) from holder, pick up by knitting 26 (28, 30) sts along armhole edge to shoulder join, then 26 (28, 30) sts along armhole edge to underarm, k6 (6, 8) rem held underarm sts—64 (68, 76) sts. Join for working in the rnd, and pm for beg of rnd. Purl one rnd. Work in Seed st for 4 rnds.

Sleeve Shaping

Dec rnd: K1, k2tog, work in patt to last 2 sts, ssk—2 sts dec'd. Rep the dec rnd every 4th rnd 11 (11, 13) more times, changing to larger dpn when there are too few sts to work with the cir—40 (44, 48) sts. Work even until sleeve measures 13 (14, 14)" (33 [35.5, 35.5] cm) from pick-up rnd. Change to smaller dpn, and work until sleeve measures 18 (19, 19)" (45.5 [48.5, 48.5] cm) from pick-up rnd. BO in pattern.

FINISHING

Buttonband

With larger 24" (60-cm) cir and beg at neck edge of left front, pick up by knitting 38 (40, 42) sts along left front to lower edge. **Next row:** (WS) Knit. Change to seed st, and work even for 15 (15, 19) rows, ending with a RS row. BO as if to knit.

Buttonhole Band

With larger 24" (60-cm) cir and beg at lower edge of right front, pick up by knitting 37 (40, 43) sts along right front to neck edge. **Next row:** (WS) Knit. Change to seed st, and work even for 6 (6, 8) rows, ending with a WS row. **Buttonhole row:** (RS) Work 3 sts in patt, yo, k2tog, [work 8 (9, 10) sts in patt, yo, k2tog] 3 times, work 2 sts in patt—4 buttonholes completed. Work in seed st for 8 (8, 10) more rows, ending with a RS row. BO as if to knit.

Neck Border

With larger 24" (60-cm) cir and beg at bound-off edge of right front buttonhole band, pick up by knitting 9 (9, 10) sts along selvedge of band, knit 7 (8, 8) sts from front neck holder, pick up by knitting 15 (17, 17) sts to back neck holder, knit 18 (20, 22) sts from back neck holder, pick up by knitting 15 (17, 17) sts to front neck holder, knit 7 (8, 8) sts from front neck holder, pick up 9 (9, 10) sts along selvedge of left front buttonband—80 (88, 92) sts. Turn, and BO all sts as if to knit on WS.

Sew buttons on buttonband to correspond to buttonholes.

Rachel Brown, master weaver and dyer in Taos, New Mexico, was one of the first to dye colorways for yarns in multiple textures. Her talents as a colorist are showcased in this jacket, which uses two strands of mohair yarn, one brushed and one loopy, to create a soft and subtle bouclé fabric in simple stockinette stitch. The hand-dyed color assures a unique garment every time.

Rachel's Jacket

"Making the simple complicated is commonplace; making the complicated simple, awesomely simple, that's creativity."

—Charles Mingus

FINISHED SIZE
40½ (44½, 47½, 51½)" (103 [113, 120.5, 131] cm) chest circumference. Jacket shown measures 44½" (113 cm). Rachel's Jacket is loose fitting (see fit guidelines on page 136).

YARN (5)
Shown here: Weaving Southwest Rio Grande Hand-Dyed Apparel Yarns Brushed Mohair (78% mohair, 13% wool, 9% nylon; about 215 yd [197 m]/3½ oz [100 g]): Camouflage, 3 (3, 4, 4) skeins.

Weaving Southwest Rio Grande Hand-Dyed Apparel Yarns Mohair Loop (78% mohair, 13% wool, 9% nylon; 215 yd [197 m]/3½ oz [100 g]): Camouflage, 3 (3, 4, 4) skeins.

Note: Jacket is knitted with one strand of each yarn held together throughout. For this jacket, the two strands together work up to a chunky gauge.

NEEDLES
Body and sleeves—size 13 (9 mm) 24" (60-cm) circular needle (cir). Sleeve shaping—size 11 (8 mm) 24" (60-cm) cir. Adjust needle size if necessary to obtain the correct gauge.

NOTIONS
Markers (m); smooth cotton scrap yarn for holders; one 1½" (3.8 cm) button

GAUGE
9 stitches and 13½ rows = 4" (10 cm) in stockinette using larger needle.

Techniques
Three-needle bind-off (page 138), pick up by knitting (page 137).

Notes
» The lower body is worked in one piece to the armholes, then the back and fronts are divided and worked separately to the shoulders.
» Work using one strand of each yarn held together throughout.

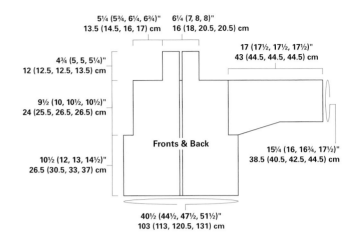

LOWER BODY

With larger cir, CO 92 (100, 108, 116) sts. **Next row:** (RS) K23 (25, 27, 29) for right front, place marker (pm) for right side, k46 (50, 54, 58) for back, pm for left side, k23 (25, 27, 29) for left front. Knit 2 rows, ending with a RS row. Change to St st, and beg with a WS purl row work even in St st until piece measures 10½ (12, 13, 14½)" (26.5 [30.5, 33, 37] cm) from CO, ending with a RS row.

Reserve Underarms and Fronts

Next row: (WS) Purl to 4 (4, 4, 5) sts past the first m, place the last 8 (8, 8, 10) sts worked on a holder for left armhole, leaving m in place to identify the center of these sts later, purl to 4 (4, 4, 5) sts past the second m, place the last 8 (8, 8, 10) sts worked (including m) on a holder for right armhole, purl to end—19 (21, 23, 24) sts each for right and left fronts; 38 (42, 46, 48) sts for back. Break yarn. Place both fronts on holders.

BACK

Rejoin yarn to 38 (42, 46, 48) back sts with RS facing. Continue in St st as established until back measures 9½ (10, 10½, 10½)" (24 [25.5, 26.5, 26.5] cm) above the underarm, ending with a RS row. Place sts on holder.

LEFT FRONT

Place 19 (21, 23, 24) held left front sts on larger cir and rejoin yarn with RS facing at armhole edge. Continue in St st as established until left front measures 9½ (10, 10½, 10½)" (24 [25.5, 26.5, 26.5] cm) above the underarm, ending with a RS row.

Left Collar

Next row: (WS) Work the first 7 (8, 9, 9) sts at neck edge for collar, then place rem 12 (13, 14, 15) sts on holder for left front shoulder. Work in St st on 7 (8, 9, 9) collar sts for 15 (16, 16, 17) rows. Bind off.

RIGHT FRONT

Place 19 (21, 23, 24) held left front sts on larger cir and rejoin yarn with RS facing at neck edge. Continue in St st as established until right front measures 9½ (10, 10½, 10½)" (24 [25.5, 26.5, 26.5] cm) above the underarm, ending with a RS row.

Right Collar

Next row: (WS) Work first 12 (13, 14, 15) sts for right front shoulder and place these sts on holder, work rem 7 (8, 9, 9) sts to end for right collar. Work in St st on 7 (8, 9, 9) collar sts for 15 (16, 16, 17) rows. Bind off.

JOIN SHOULDERS

With RS of pieces touching and WS facing outward, join 12 (13, 14, 15) front and back shoulder sts using the three-needle bind-off method—14 (16, 18, 18) sts rem on holder for center back neck.

SLEEVES

Note: Stitches for the sleeves are picked up around the armhole and worked back and forth in rows down to the wrist, then the sleeve seams are sewn. Using larger cir, beg at marker in center of held underarm sts, k4 (4, 4, 5) from holder, pick up by knitting 19 (20, 21, 21) sts along armhole edge to shoulder join, then 19 (20, 21, 21) sts along armhole edge to underarm, k4 (4, 4, 5) rem held underarm sts—46 (48, 50, 52) sts. Work in St st for 7 (7, 7, 9) rows, beg and ending with a WS row.

Sleeve Shaping

Dec row: (RS) K1, k2tog, knit to last 3 sts, ssk, k1—2 sts dec'd. Rep the dec row every 4th row 2 more times—40 (42, 44, 46) sts. Work even in St st for 8 (12, 12, 12) more rows. Change to smaller cir. Work even until piece measures 17 (17½, 17½, 17½)" (43 [44.5, 44.5, 44.5] cm) from pick-up row, ending with a RS row. Knit 2 rows. BO as if to knit. Sew sleeve seam.

FINISHING

Collar

Rejoin yarn to 14 (16, 18, 18) held back neck sts and BO these sts. Sew bound-off ends of right and left collars tog.

Mark center back neck. Matching collar seam to center back, sew one selvedge of each collar to bound-off back neck edge, working from shoulder to center back and easing to fit.

Front Band

With larger cir and RS facing, beg at lower edge of right front pick up by knitting 48 (52, 55, 58) sts up along right front to center back collar seam, then 48 (52, 55, 58) sts along left front to lower edge—96 (104, 110, 116) sts. Knit 2 rows. Using a larger needle if necessary, BO off loosely as if to knit until 5 sts rem on left needle and 1 st rem on right needle. **Button loop:** On right needle, [yo, pass 1st st on right needle over yo] 5 times—button loop completed; 1 st rem on right needle. BO rem sts to end.

Sew button to correspond with loop about 3½" (9 cm) in from left front edge as shown in photograph above.

Like traditional Andean garments made from alpaca yarn, Cusco is soft, lightweight, and warm. The construction, two rectangles, makes it among the simplest of jackets. Cusco is a shape shifter however, assuming a bolero structure when put on. Worn open or closed, with a pin or with the collar draped, this style is magical.

Cusco

"From the tree of silence hangs the fruit of tranquility."

—Peruvian proverb

FINISHED SIZE
69 (78)" (175.5 [198] cm) chest circumference. Jacket shown measures 69" (175.5 cm). Cusco is loose fitting (see fit guidelines on page 136). **Note:** Because of the unusual shape and drapey fit of this garment, Size A will fit a size small to medium frame with about a 30" to 38" (76 to 96.5 cm) chest, and Size B will fit a medium to large frame with about a 40" to 48" (101.5 to 122 cm) chest.

YARN (5)
Shown here: Cascade Pastaza (50% llama, 50% wool; 132 yd [121 m]/100 g): #065 Claret, 7 (8) skeins.

NEEDLES
Size 9 (5.5 mm): 24" and 16" (60- and 40-cm) circular needles (cir). Adjust needle size if necessary to obtain the correct gauge.

NOTIONS
Markers (m); smooth cotton scrap yarn for provisional cast-on.

GAUGE
14 stitches and 22 rows = 4" (10 cm) in stockinette.

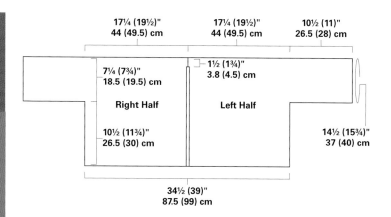

17¼ (19½)" 44 (49.5) cm — 17¼ (19½)" 44 (49.5) cm — 10½ (11)" 26.5 (28) cm

7¼ (7¾)" 18.5 (19.5) cm — 1½ (1¾)" 3.8 (4.5) cm

Right Half — Left Half

10½ (11¾)" 26.5 (30) cm

14½ (15¾)" 37 (40) cm

34½ (39)" 87.5 (99) cm

LEFT HALF

Using a provisional method and longer cir, CO 125 (137) sts. Beg and ending with a WS purl row, work in St st for 15 (19) rows. *Work Rows 1–26 of Lace chart at right, then work 14 (18) rows in St st; rep from * once more—95 (107) rows total from beg; piece measures about 17¼ (19½)" (49.5 [50] cm) from CO.

Join the Sides

Fold piece in half with WS tog and RS facing outward. Beg at the selvedges (lower edge of garment), join the first 37 (41) sts of each half using the three-needle bind-off method—51 (55) sts rem: 1st on right needle after last bind-off and 50 (54) live sts around armhole. Do not break yarn. The bind-off ridge will form a decorative welt on the outside of the garment.

Sleeve

Place 51 (55) sleeve sts on shorter cir. Pm between the last bind-off st and first live armhole st, and join for working in the rnd; single bind-off st will be the last st of the rnd.

Next rnd: *Yo, k2tog; rep from * to last st, k1. Work in St st (knit all sts every rnd) until sleeve measures 10½ (11)" (26.5 [28] cm) from side joining row. BO all sts and allow bound-off edge of cuff to roll up naturally to the RS.

RIGHT HALF

Work as for left half.

JOIN AT CENTER BACK

Carefully remove provisional cast-on from 68 (75) sts along center back edge of both pieces and place sts on longer cir. Bring the needle tips tog with WS of pieces tog and RS facing outward. Beg at lower back edge and working with shorter cir, join 68 (75) back sts of each half tog using the three-needle bind-off method.

FINISHING
Front Edge

Remove provisional cast-on from rem 57 (62) sts of each half and place all sts on longer cir for front edge—114 (124) sts. With RS facing, rejoin yarn to lower edge of right front. BO all sts and allow bound-off front edge to roll naturally to the RS.

Lower Edge

With longer cir and beg at lower corner of left front, pick up by knitting 62 (68) along lower edge of left front to left side join, 62 (68) sts from side join to center back, 62 (68) sts from center back to right side join, and 62 (68) sts from side join to right front edge—248 (272) sts. Beg WS, knit 2 rows. BO loosely as if to knit on WS. **Tip:** BO using a larger needle to keep bind-off loose and flexible.

Lightly tack rolled front edges to lower edge at bottom front corners.

	k on RS; p on WS
o	yo
∕	k2tog
＼	ssk
∧	sl 2 sts as if to k2tog, k1, pass 2 slipped sts over
	pattern repeat

Lace

(Chart, RS rows 1–25)

Note: Only RS pattern rows are charted.

Purl all even-numbered WS rows, including 26.

Rich brown yarn brings back warm childhood memories of walks taken with my mother. She wore her brown tweed jacket, the stylish one she had designed and sewn herself. In soft yarn and two-by-two ribbing, The Wrapper can be loosely draped or snugly wrapped. Showcase a shawl pin, roll the cuffs, spread the collar, and take a long walk.

The Wrapper

"Take, if you must, this little bag of dreams, unloose the cord, and they will wrap you round."

—William Butler Yeats

FINISHED SIZE
40 (44, 48)" (101.5 [112, 122] cm) chest circumference. Jacket shown measures 44" (112 cm). The Wrapper is standard fitting (see fit guidelines on page 136).

YARN 3
Shown here: Schulana Tweed-Lux (85% wool, 10% silk, 5% cashmere; 109 yds [100 m]/50 g): #3 Chocolate, 12 (15, 17) balls.

NEEDLES
Body and sleeves—2 size 5 (3.75 mm) 24" (60-cm) circular (cir) and 1 size 5 (3.75 mm) 16" (40-cm) cir. Cuff—size 5 (3.75 mm) double-pointed (dpn). Waist shaping—size 4 (3.5 mm) 24" (60-cm) cir. Adjust needle size if necessary to obtain the correct gauge.

NOTIONS
Safety pin; markers (m); smooth cotton scrap yarn for holders.

GAUGE
18 stitches and 26 rows = 4" (10 cm) in stockinette using larger needle; 24 stitches and 32 rows = 4" (10 cm) in K2, P2 Rib using larger needle.

Techniques

Backward-loop increase (page 137), three-needle bind-off (page 138), pick up by knitting (page 137).

Stitch Guide

K2, P2 Rib Worked Flat
(multiple of 4 sts, plus 2)

Row 1: (RS) P2, *k2, p2; rep from *.
Row 2: K2, *p2, k2; rep from *.
Rep Rows 1 and 2 for patt.

K2, P2 Rib Worked Circularly
(multiple of 4 sts, plus 3)

All Rnds: P3, *k2, p2; rep from *.
Rep this rnd for patt. **Note:** Each rnd deliberately begins and ends with purl sts, with 1 extra purl st at the start of the rnd.

Notes

» The lower body is worked in one piece to the armholes, then the back and fronts are divided and worked separately to the shoulders.

» The body is slightly shaped by switching to a smaller needle at the waistline. This shaping can be eliminated for a roomier fit.

» Place a safety pin on the RS of the fabric to distinguish it from the WS.

LOWER BODY

With larger 24" (60-cm) needle, CO 242 (270, 294) sts. Beg K2, P2 Rib Worked Flat (see Stitch Guide), placing markers (pm) in Row 1 as foll: Work 61 (69, 75) sts in patt for right front, pm for right side, work 120 (132, 144) sts in patt for back, pm for left side, work 61 (69, 75) sts in

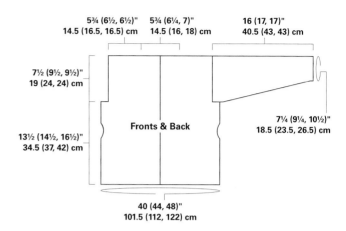

5¾ (6½, 6½)" 14.5 (16.5, 16.5) cm   5¾ (6¼, 7)" 14.5 (16, 18) cm   16 (17, 17)" 40.5 (43, 43) cm

7½ (9½, 9½)" 19 (24, 24) cm

Fronts & Back

7¼ (9¼, 10½)" 18.5 (23.5, 26.5) cm

13½ (14½, 16½)" 34.5 (37, 42) cm

40 (44, 48)" 101.5 (112, 122) cm

patt for left front. Continue even in patt until piece measures 7½ (8, 9)" (19 [20.5, 23] cm) from CO. If waist shaping is desired, change to smaller 24" (60-cm) cir and continue in patt until body measures 10 (11½, 12½)" (25.5 [29, 31.5] cm) from CO. Change back to larger cir. Work even until body measures 13½ (14½, 16½) (34.5 [37, 42] cm) from CO, ending with a RS row.

Reserve Underarms and Fronts

Next row: (WS) Work in patt as established to 8 (8, 12) sts past the first side marker (m), place the last 16 (16, 24) sts worked on holder for left armhole, leaving m in place to identify the center of these sts later, work in patt to 8 (8, 12) sts past the second m, place the last 16 (16, 24) sts worked (including m) on holder for the right armhole, work in patt to end for right front—53 (61, 63) sts each for right and left fronts; 104 (116, 120) sts for back. Break yarn. Place both fronts on holders.

Back

Rejoin yarn to 104 (116, 120) back sts on needle with RS facing. Continue in established patt until back measures 7½ (9½, 9½)" (19 [24, 24] cm) above underarm, ending with a RS row. Place sts on holder.

LEFT FRONT

Place 53 (61, 63) left front sts on larger 24" (60-cm) cir and rejoin yarn with RS facing at armhole edge. Continue in established patt until the front measures 7½ (9½, 9½)" (19 [24, 24] cm) above underarm, ending with a RS row. Place sts on holder.

RIGHT FRONT

Place 53 (61, 63) right front sts on larger 24" (60-cm) cir and rejoin yarn with RS facing at neck edge. Continue in established patt until the front measures 7½ (9½, 9½)" (19 [24, 24] cm) above underarm, ending with a RS row. Place sts on holder.

JOIN SHOULDERS

With WS of pieces touching and RS facing outward, join 35 (39, 39) front and back shoulder sts using the three-needle bind-off method, dec sts by half during the BO to prevent shoulders from flaring as foll: Knit 1 st from each needle tog, *then knit 2 sts from each needle tog (2 sts from front needle, 2 sts from back needle), BO 1 st; rep from * until 18 (22, 24) sts rem on holder for each front neck, and 34 (38, 42) sts rem on holder for center back neck. The bind-off ridge will form a decorative welt on the outside of the garment.

SLEEVES

Notes: Sleeves are worked in the round from cuffs upward, then attached to the body by binding off the live sleeve sts tog with sts picked up around the armhole opening using the three-needle bind-off method. With dpn, CO 43 (55, 63) sts. Join for working in the rnd, and pm for beg of rnd. Work in K2, P2 Rib Worked Circularly (see Stitch Guide) for 5 rnds. **Inc rnd:** Using the backward-loop method for all incs, p1, inc 1, work in patt to end, inc 1—2 sts inc'd. **Notes:** Keep the first st of every rnd as p1 throughout, work the shaping increases on each side of this purl st, and incorporate the new sts into established rib patt. Rep the inc rnd every 6th rnd 3 (16, 16) more times, changing to 16" (40-cm) cir when there are too

many sts for dpn, then every 5th round 20 (6, 6) times—91 (101, 109) sts. Continue even in patt until piece measures 16 (17, 17)" (40.5 [43, 43] cm) from CO.

Set up Armholes and Attach Sleeves

Note: Leave underarm holder strings in place until after the underarm sts have been attached, then remove holders. With largest 24" (60-cm) cir and RS facing, beg at m in center of held underarm sts, k8 (8, 12) from holder, pick up by knitting 37 (42, 42) sts along armhole edge to shoulder join, then 1 st in join, then 37 (42, 42) sts along armhole edge to underarm, k8 (8, 12) rem held underarm sts—91 (101, 109) sts. With WS of pieces touching and RS facing outward, beg at underarm m, join 91 (101, 109) live sts at top of sleeve to 91 (101, 109) sts picked up around armhole using the three-needle bind-off method.

FINISHING
Collar

Place 18 (22, 24) right front sts on larger cir and rejoin yarn with RS facing at neck edge. **Next row:** (RS) Working in established patt, work 18 (22, 24) right front neck sts, pick up by knitting 2 (2, 0) sts at shoulder join, work 34 (38, 42) back neck sts, pick up by knitting 2 (2, 0) sts at shoulder join, work 18 (22, 24) left front sts—74 (86, 90) sts. Continue working established patt back and forth in rows until collar measures 4" (10 cm) from pick-up row. BO in pattern.

Every moment of light and dark is a miracle.

—Walt Whitman

Contrast

Light and dark, warm and cool, strong or subtle, the play of contrast defines pattern. In knitting, color patterns are often practical as well as beautiful, adding an extra layer of fiber for warmth and comfort.

The Salish, a First Nations people on Vancouver Island, have created graphically stunning knitted jackets for 100 years. Taught to knit by early Scottish settlers, these artisans applied their talents to the creation of the handspun, shawl-collared jackets that are worldwide favorites. In tribute to this blending of cultures, Northwest Celtic incorporates Celtic designs into the Salish-style sweater.

Northwest Celtic

"Say only a little but say it well."

—Celtic Proverb

FINISHED SIZE

Size A: 48" (122 cm) chest circumference
Size B: 51" (129.5 cm) chest circumference
Size C: 55" (139.5 cm) chest circumference
Jacket shown measures 51" (129.5 cm). Northwest Celtic is oversize (see fit guidelines on page 136).

YARN 5

Brown Sheep Company Lamb's Pride Bulky (85% wool, 15% mohair; 125 yd [114 m]/4 oz [113 g]): #M-06 Deep Charcoal (MC), 9 (9, 10) skeins; #M-03 Grey Heather (CC), 3 (3, 4) skeins.

NEEDLES

Size A: Body and sleeves—size 10 (6 mm) 24" and 16" (60- and 40-cm) circular needles (cir) and set of 4 double-pointed (dpn). Body plain stockinette shaped section—size 9 (5.5 mm) 24" (60-cm) cir. Cuffs—size 8 (5 mm) set of 4 dpn. Body lower edge, collar, and front bands—size 7 (4.5 mm) 24" (60-cm) cir.

Size B: Body and sleeves—size 11 (8 mm) 24" and 16" (60- and 40-cm) circular needles (cir) and set of 4 double-pointed (dpn). Body plain stockinette shaped section—size 10 (6 mm) 24" (60-cm) cir. Cuffs—size 9 (5.5 mm) set of 4 dpn. Body lower edge, collar and front bands—size 8 (5 mm) 24" (60-cm) cir.

Size C: Body and sleeves—size 13 (9 mm) 24" and 16" (60- and 40-cm) circular needles (cir) and set of 4 double-pointed (dpn). Body plain stockinette shaped section—size 11 (8 mm) 24" (60-cm) cir. Cuffs—size 10 (6 mm) set of 4 dpn. Body lower edge, collar and front bands—size 9 (5.5 mm) 24" (60-cm) cir.
Adjust needle size if necessary to obtain the correct gauge (see Notes next page).

Techniques

Steeks (page 141), chart reading (page 139), two-color knitting (page 140), three-needle bind-off (page 138), backward-loop increase (page 137), pick up by knitting (page 137), short rows (page 138).

Notes

» The size of the jacket is determined by the needle size—the larger sizes are made using larger needles. For this reason, doing a gauge swatch is very important!

» The body is worked in the round to the shoulders with steeks for the front opening and armholes.

» The two-color stockinette sections are worked using the largest needle (the one used for the swatch), and the plain, one-color sections of the body (but not the sleeves) are worked using a needle one size smaller to create subtle shaping. Change needle sizes where indicated in the pattern, or continue with the same size needle to eliminate this shaping for a roomier fit.

NOTIONS

Markers (m); smooth cotton scrap yarn for holders; five 1" (2.5 cm) buttons.

GAUGE

Size A: 15 stitches and 18⅔ rows = 4" (10 cm) in two-color stockinette using largest needle.

Size B: 14 stitches and 17⅓ rows = 4" (10 cm) in two-color stockinette using largest needle.

Size C: 13 stitches and 16 rows = 4" (10 cm) in two-color stockinette using largest needle.

Work your gauge swatch from the 30-st marked section of Chart 1.

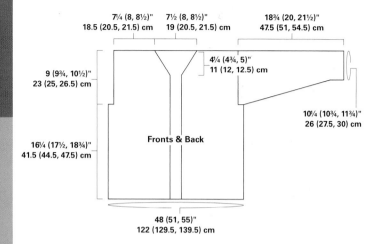

7¼ (8, 8½)" 18.5 (20.5, 21.5) cm — 7½ (8, 8½)" 19 (20.5, 21.5) cm — 18¾ (20, 21½)" 47.5 (51, 54.5) cm

4¼ (4¾, 5)" 11 (12, 12.5) cm

9 (9¾, 10½)" 23 (25, 26.5) cm

10¼ (10¾, 11¾)" 26 (27.5, 30) cm

Fronts & Back

16¼ (17½, 18¾)" 41.5 (44.5, 47.5) cm

48 (51, 55)" 122 (129.5, 139.5) cm

BODY

Lower Border

With MC and smallest 24" (60-cm) needle, CO 172 sts for all sizes. Working back and forth in rows, work in garter st (knit all sts every row) for 10 rows.

Steek and Join

Place a marker (pm) on the right needle, then use the attached working yarn to CO 3 sts onto the right needle for center front steek, pm—175 sts. Join for working in the rnd, being sure that your sts are not twisted, by knitting the first st on the left needle; this st becomes the first st of each rnd and is also the first st of the right front, after the center front steek sts. **Next rnd:** Knit until there are 41 right front sts, pm for right side, k90 for back, pm for left side, k41 for left front, slip steek m, work 3 steek sts.

Begin Color Patterns

Change to largest 24" (60-cm) needle. Work Rnd 1 of Chart 1, beg and ending where indicated for lower body as foll: Work 1 st before patt rep box, rep entire 38-st patt rep

4 times, work 19 sts after patt rep box once, slip steek m, work 3 steek sts. Work Rnds 2–26 of chart. Work Rnd 1 of Chart 2, beg and ending where indicated for lower body, and pm for center back as foll: Work 5 sts before first patt rep box once, rep first 8-st patt rep box 9 times, work 9 sts, pm where indicated for center back, work 9 sts, rep second 8-st patt rep box 9 times, work 5 sts to end of chart, work 3 steek sts. Continue in established patt until Rnd 14 of chart has been completed. If working body shaping, change to 24" (60-cm) cir one size smaller than largest needle, or continue with largest cir if omitting shaping. With MC, knit 28 rnds—piece measures about 16¼ (17½, 18¾)" (41.5 [44.5, 47.5] cm) from CO.

Steek Armholes and Reserve Underarms

Next rnd: Knit to 4 sts before right side m, place the next 8 sts on holder for right armhole, leaving m in place to identify the center of these sts later, *pm, CO 3 sts onto right needle for steek, pm,* knit to 4 sts before left side m, place the next 8 sts worked (including m) on holder for left armhole; rep from * to * once more for left armhole steek, knit to end—165 sts total; 37 sts each for right and left fronts; 82 sts for back; 3 sts in each steek at center front and both armholes. Change back to largest cir if necessary. Work Rnd 1 from Chart 1 as foll: For right front, work 37 sts beg and ending where indicated; work 3 armhole steek sts; for back, beg where indicated for back work last 32 sts of patt rep once, work entire 38-st patt rep once, work 12 sts after patt rep once; work 3 armhole steek sts; for left front, work 37 sts beg and ending where indicated; work 3 center front steek sts. Continue in patt from chart as established until Rnd 22 of chart has been completed.

Neck Shaping

Tip: Place markers in the knitted fabric itself (and not on the needle) on each side of the steek to indicate start of neck shaping.

Chart 1

30 sts for swatch

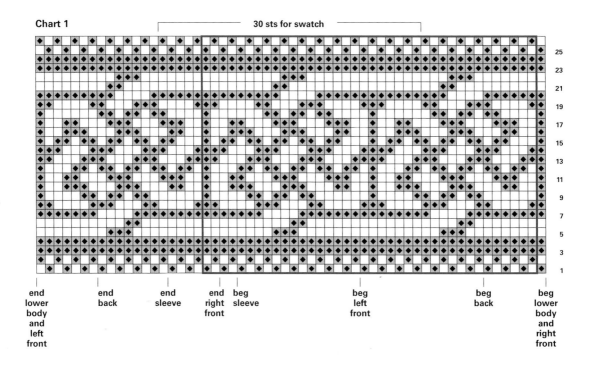

25
23
21
19
17
15
13
11
9
7
5
3
1

end
lower
body
and
left
front

end
back

end
sleeve

end
right
front

beg
sleeve

beg
left
front

beg
back

beg
lower
body
and
right
front

Chart 2

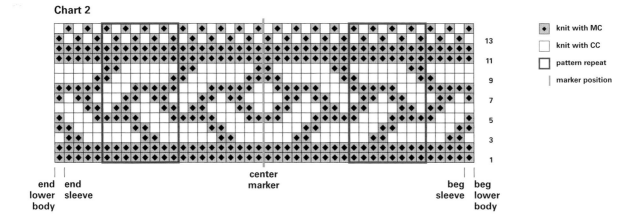

13
11
9
7
5
3
1

end
lower
body

end
sleeve

center
marker

beg
sleeve

beg
lower
body

◆ knit with MC

☐ knit with CC

☐ pattern repeat

| marker position

Continue in patt from chart, working neck shaping on each side of center front steek sts as foll:

Rnds 23 and 25: (Dec rnd) K1, ssk work in patt to last 6 sts, k2tog, k1, work 3 steek sts—2 sts dec'd in each rnd; 35 sts each for right and left fronts after Rnd 25.

Rnds 24 and 26: Work even.

Using MC only, rep the dec rnd on the next rnd, then every other rnd 7 more times—145 sts total; 27 sts each for right and left fronts; 82 sts for back; 3 sts in each steek at center front and both armholes; piece measures about 9 (9¾, 10½)" (23 [25, 26.5] cm) above underarms. Place sts (including markers) on holder.

STITCHING AND CUTTING

Machine stitch and cut the steeks for the center front opening and both armholes.

JOIN SHOULDERS

With WS of pieces touching and RS facing outward, join 27 front and back shoulder sts using the three-needle bind-off method—28 sts rem on holder for center back neck. Leave back neck m in place to identify the center of these sts later—14 sts on each side of m. The bind-off ridge will form a decorative welt on the outside of the garment.

SLEEVES

Note: Sleeves are worked in the round from cuffs upward, then attached to the body by binding off the live sleeve sts tog with sts picked up around the armhole opening using the three-needle bind-off method. With MC and smaller dpn, CO 30 sts. Join for working in the rnd, and pm for beg of rnd. Next rnd: *K1, p1; rep from * to end. Continue in ribbing as established until piece measures 2½" (6.5 cm). Change to larger dpn. Knit 1 rnd, inc 8 sts evenly spaced—38 sts. Knit 4 more rnds. **Inc rnd:** Using the backward-loop method for all incs, k1, inc 1, knit to end, inc 1—2 sts inc'd. Continue in St st, rep inc rnd every 4th rnd 3 more times, changing to 16" (40-cm) cir in largest size when there are too many sts to fit on the dpn—46 sts.

Begin Color Patterns

Note: While working sleeve, the inc rnd will be repeated every 4th rnd a total of 13 more times as given below. Incorporate the new sts into established chart patts. Work Rnd 1 of Chart 1, beg and ending where indicated for sleeve as foll: Work last 4 sts of patt rep box once, work entire 38-st patt rep once, work 4 sts after patt rep box once. Work Rnds 2–26 of Chart 1, inc 2 sts as for inc rnd on Rnds 4, 8, 12, 16, 20, and 24—58 sts after completing Chart 1. Work Rnd 1 of Chart 2, beg and ending where indicated for sleeve as foll: Work 4 sts before first patt rep box once, rep first 8-st patt rep box 2 times, work next 9 sts once, pm for center of sleeve, work next 9 sts once, rep second 8-st patt rep box 2 times, work 4 sts after second patt rep box. Work Rnds 2–14 of chart in established patt, increasing on Rnds 2, 6, 10, and 14—66 sts. With MC only, knit 18 rnds, working inc rnd every 4th rnd 3 more times as established—72 sts; piece measures about 18¾ (20, 21½)" (47.5 [51, 54.5] cm) from CO. Place sts on holder or leave on needle if attaching to body immediately.

Set up Armholes and Attach Sleeves

Note: Leave underarm holder strings in place until after the underarm sts have been attached, then remove holders. With largest 24" (60-cm) cir and RS facing, beg at m in center of held underarm sts, k4 from holder, pick up by knitting 32 sts along armhole edge to shoulder join, then 32 sts along armhole edge to underarm, k4 rem held underarm sts—72 sts. With RS of pieces touching and WS facing outward, beg at underarm m, join 72 live sts at top of sleeve to 72 sts picked up around armhole using the three-needle bind-off method.

FINISHING
Collar and Front Bands

Note: The collar and front bands are knitted in one piece in garter st with short-row shaping for the collar. With MC and smallest 24" (60-cm) cir, with RS facing and beg at lower edge of right front, pick up by knitting 53 sts along right front to beg of neck shaping, pm, pick up 21 sts along right neck edge to shoulder join, knit first 14 held back neck sts, sl center back neck m, knit last 14 held back neck sts, pick up 21 sts along left front neck to beg of neck shaping, pm, pick up 53 sts along left front to lower edge—176 sts; 70 sts between neck shaping m; 35 sts on each side of center back m. Knit 1 WS row.

Collar Shaping

Short-row 1: (RS): Knit to center back neck m, sl m, k3, wrap next st and turn (WT).

Short-row 2: (WS): Knit to m, sl m, k3, WT—first short-row set completed; wrapped sts are the 4th sts on each side of center back m.

Short-rows 3 and 4: Knit to previously wrapped st, knit wrapped st, WT—second short-row set completed; wrapped sts are the 5th sts on each side of center back m.

Note: If you are accustomed to working wrapped sts tog with their wraps, it is not necessary to do so in garter st; simply knit each wrapped st as you come to it.

Short–rows 5–64: Rep Short-rows 3 and 4 thirty more times, working each new wrapped st immediately after the previous wrapped st and 1 st farther out from the center back m in each set of short-rows, and ending with a WS row at right front neck shaping m—last wrapped st at each side is st next to neck shaping m.

Front Borders

Next 2 rows: Knit to end—all sts have been worked. Continue in garter st for 4 more rows, ending with a WS row.

Buttonhole row: (RS) K3, yo, k2tog, *k10, yo, k2tog; rep from * 3 more times, knit to end of row—5 buttonholes completed. Continue in garter st for 6 more rows, ending with a RS row. BO loosely as if to knit. **Tip:** BO using a larger needle to keep bind-off loose and flexible.

Sew buttons into place on left front to correspond to buttonholes.

The texture and color of Dakota on the Side are achieved by using slip stitches, a simple two-color knitting technique that requires only one color per row. Slipping stitches pulls them up from the row below to add color and texture to the knitted fabric. The jacket is styled with Asian flair, and with its vertical lines, is very flattering.

Dakota on the Side

"Love yourself, get outside yourself and take action, focus on the solution, be at peace."

—Sioux Proverb

FINISHED SIZE

Size A: 49" (124.5 cm) chest circumference

Size B: 52" (132 cm) chest circumference

Size C: 55" (139.5 cm) chest circumference

Jacket shown measures 52" (132 cm). Dakota is oversize (see fit guidelines on page 136).

YARN (3)

Shown here: Cheryl Oberle's Dancing Colors Hand-dyed (45% merino, 55% mohair; 485 yd [443 m]/8 oz [227 g]): Evening (MC), 2 hanks.

Shown here: Brown Sheep Company Nature Spun Sport (100% wool; 184 yd [168 m]/50 g): 601 Pepper (CC), 8 balls.

NEEDLES

Size A: Body and sleeves—size 4 (3.5 mm) 24" and 16" (60- and 40-cm) circular needles (cir). Lower border—size 2 (3 mm) 24" (60-cm) cir. Cuffs and front band—size 1 (2.5 mm) 16" and 29" (40- and 74-cm) cir.

Size B: Body and sleeves—size 5 (3.75 mm) 24" and 16" (60- and 40-cm) circular needles (cir). Lower border—size 3 (3.25 mm) 24" (60-cm) cir. Cuffs and front band—size 2 (3 mm) 16" and 29" (40- and 74-cm) cir.

Size C: Body and sleeves—size 6 (4 mm) 24" and 16" (60- and 40-cm) circular needles (cir). Lower border—size 4 (3.5 mm) 24" (60-cm) cir. Cuffs and front band—size 3 (3.25 mm) 16" and 29" (40- and 74-cm) cir.

Adjust needle size if necessary to obtain the correct gauge.

NOTIONS

Markers (m); smooth cotton scrap yarn for provisional cast-on and holders.

GAUGE

Size A: 24 stitches and 32 rows = 4" (10 cm) in stockinette using largest needle; 24 sts and 36 rows = 4" (10 cm) in Dakota Pattern Worked Flat using largest needle.

Size B: 22 stitches and 30 rows = 4" (10 cm) in stockinette using largest needle; 22 sts and 34 rows = 4" (10 cm) in Dakota Pattern Worked Flat using largest needle.

Size C: 20 stitches and 28 rows = 4" (10 cm) in stockinette using largest needle; 20 sts and 32 rows = 4" (10 cm) in Dakota Pattern Worked Flat using largest needle.

Techniques

Provisional cast-on (page 137), slip stitches (page 141), three-needle bind-off (page 138).

Stitch Guide

Dakota Pattern Worked Flat
(odd number of sts)

Rows 1, 3, and 5: (RS) With MC, knit.

Rows 2 and 4: (WS) With MC, purl.

Row 6: (WS) With CC, *k1, sl 1 as if to purl with yarn in back (pwise wyb); rep from * to last st, k1.

Row 7: (RS) With CC, *k1, sl 1 pwise wyb; rep from *, to last st, k1.

Row 8: (WS) With CC, *p1, sl 1 pwise with yarn in front (wyf); rep from *, to last st, p1.

Rows 9, 11, and 13: (RS) With CC, knit.

Rows 10 and 12: (WS) With CC, purl.

Row 14: (WS) With MC, *k1, sl 1 pwise wyb; rep from *, to last st, k1.

Row 15: (RS) With MC, *k1, sl 1 pwise wyb; rep from *, to last st, k1.

Row 16: (WS) With MC, *p1, sl 1 pwise wyf; rep from *, to last st, p1.

Rep Rows 1–16 for patt.

Dakota Pattern Worked Circularly
(even number of sts)

Rnds 1–5: With MC, knit.

Rnd 6: With CC, *p1, sl 1 pwise wyf; rep from *.

Rnds 7 and 8: With CC, *k1, sl 1 pwise wyb; rep from *.

Rnds 9–13: With CC, knit.

Rnd 14: With MC, *p1, sl 1 pwise wyf; rep from *.

Rnds 15 and 16: With MC, *k1, sl 1 pwise wyb; rep from *.

Rep Rnds 1–16 for patt.

Seed Stitch Worked Flat
(odd number of stitches)

All Rows: *K1, p1; rep from * to last st, k1.

Rep this row for patt.

Seed Stitch Worked Circularly
(even number of stitches)

Rnd 1: *K1, p1; rep from *.

Rnd 2: *P1, k1; rep from *.

Rep Rnds 1 and 2 for patt.

Notes

» The size of the jacket is determined by the needle size—the larger sizes are made using larger needles. For this reason, doing a gauge swatch is very important!

» Each half of the body is worked flat from the center back outward. The two completed halves are joined at center back with a three-needle bind-off. The sleeves are worked circularly down from the armholes, and the cuffs and front borders are worked in seed stitch.

» Instead of cutting the yarn at each color change, carry the yarn not in use loosely up to where it is needed next. To prevent long loops of carried yarn inside the garment, twist the carried yarn around the working yarn every few rows or rounds.

» The body lengths shown on the schematic do not include the lower border, which will add about 1" to the length of the garment.

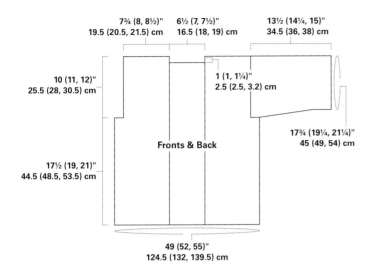

7¾ (8, 8½)"
19.5 (20.5, 21.5) cm

6½ (7, 7½)"
16.5 (18, 19) cm

13½ (14¼, 15)"
34.5 (36, 38) cm

10 (11, 12)"
25.5 (28, 30.5) cm

1 (1, 1¼)"
2.5 (2.5, 3.2) cm

Fronts & Back

17¾ (19¼, 21¼)"
45 (49, 54) cm

17½ (19, 21)"
44.5 (48.5, 53.5) cm

49 (52, 55)"
124.5 (132, 139.5) cm

RIGHT HALF

Note: RS rows are worked from the lower edge of the garment up to the neck/shoulder line; WS rows are worked from the neck/shoulder line down to the lower edge.

Right Back

Using a provisional method and 24" (60-cm) cir in largest size, CO 159 sts for all sizes. Work Rows 1–16 of Dakota Pattern Worked Flat, then work Rows 1–13 once more—29 rows total. At the end of Row 13, CO 6 sts for right back neck shaping—165 sts.

Shoulder and Armhole Shaping

Continue in established patt until 96 rows (6 full patt reps) of patt have been completed, then work Rows 1 and 2 once more—98 rows total. **Next row:** (RS, Row 3 of patt) Work 105 sts in patt, place rem 60 sts on holder for right back armhole. Continue in established patt on 105 sts for right side for 29 more rows, ending with Row 16 of patt—128 rows total; 8 full repeats of patt completed.

Next row: (RS, Row 1 of patt) Work to end of row, break yarn. Use a provisional method to CO 60 sts at the end of this row for right front armhole—165 sts.

Right Front

Next row: (WS, Row 2 of patt) Rejoin yarn to beg of new CO sts with WS facing, work in established patt to end. Continue in patt until 192 rows (12 full patt reps) have been completed, then work Rows 1–5 once more, ending with a RS row—197 rows total from CO. Place all sts on holder.

LEFT HALF

Note: RS rows are worked from the neck/shoulder line down to the lower edge of the garment; WS rows are worked from the lower edge up to the neck/shoulder line.

Left Back

Using a provisional method and 24" (60-cm) cir in largest size, CO 159 sts. Work Rows 1–16 of Dakota Pattern Worked Flat, then work Rows 1–12 once more—28 rows total. At the end of Row 12, CO 6 sts for left back neck shaping—165 sts.

Shoulder and Armhole Shaping

Continue in established patt until 96 rows (6 full patt reps) of patt have been completed, then work Rows 1 and 2 once more—98 rows total. **Next row:** (RS, Row 3 of patt) Break yarn and place first 60 sts on holder for left back armhole, rejoin yarn with RS facing and work rem 105 sts in patt to end. Continue in established patt on 105 sts for left side for 29 more rows, ending Row 16 of patt—128 rows total; 8 full repeats of patt completed. Break yarn. **Next row:** (RS, Row 1 of patt) Use a provisional method to CO 60 sts at the beg of this row for left front armhole, rejoin yarn to beg of new CO sts, work in patt across all sts—165 sts.

Left Front

Beg with WS Row 2, continue in established patt until 192 rows (12 full patt reps) have been completed. Work Rows 1–5 once more, ending with a RS row—197 rows total. Place all sts on holder.

JOIN CENTER BACK AND SEW SHOULDERS

Carefully remove provisional cast-on from 159 sts along center back edge of both pieces and place sts on separate needles. Hold needles with WS of pieces tog and RS facing outward. With MC and largest-size needle, beg at lower back edge, join 159 back sts of each half tog using the three-needle bind-off method. The bind-off ridge will form a decorative welt on the outside of the garment. Sew shoulder seams, matching solid-color stripes.

LOWER BORDER

Using CC and 24" (60-cm) cir in middle size, pick up by knitting 262 sts along entire lower edge of garment (about 2 sts for every 3 rows). Beg with a WS purl row, work in St st for 20 rows. BO very loosely. Better yet, thread live sts on a doubled strand of CC to secure, which will allow sts to expand most freely while still being secured inside the rolled edge. Let the border roll naturally to the RS, then tack roll in place loosely across its upper edge as shown.

SLEEVES

Note: Stitches for the sleeves are picked up around the armhole, and the sleeves are worked down to the wrist in Dakota Pattern Worked Circularly. Using MC and 16" (40-cm) cir in largest size, beg in center of underarm section pick up by knitting 8 sts along underarm selvedge, k120 armhole sts from holders, pick up by knitting 8 sts along underarm selvedge to end in center of underarm—136 sts. Pm and join for working in the rnd. Next rnd: (counts as Rnd 5 of patt) Knit. Beg with Rnd 6, continue in patt for 19 more rnds, ending with Rnd 8.

Sleeve Shaping

Next rnd: Rnd 9 of patt K1, k2tog, knit to last 2 sts, ssk—2 sts dec'd. Continue in established patt, work dec rnd every 8 rnds 9 more times—116 sts.

Cuff

Change to 16" (40-cm) cir in smallest size and CC. **Next rnd:** Knit, dec 10 sts evenly spaced—106 sts. **Note:** Cuff continues in seed st using two strands of CC held together. Join a second strand of CC, and with two strands held tog work in Seed Stitch Worked Circularly for 32 rounds. BO in patt.

FINISHING
Front Band

Using a single strand of CC and 29" (74-cm) cir in smallest size, with RS facing and beg at lower edge of right front pick up by knitting 3 sts from selvedge of rolled border, place 165 held right front sts on needle and knit them dec 19 sts evenly spaced (149 sts on needle), pick up by knitting 40 sts across back neck, place 165 held left front sts on needle and knit them dec 19 sts evenly spaced (335 sts on needle); pick up by knitting 3 sts from selvedge of rolled border—338 sts. Join a second strand of CC, and with two strands held tog work in Seed Stitch Worked Flat for 32 rows, ending with a RS row. BO loosely in patt. **Tip:** BO using a larger needle to keep bind-off loose and flexible.

The word "bodice" was originally the sixteenth century word for "bodies" and today means a close-fitting women's vest. A woven bodice with knitted sleeves is often found in the folk costumes of Scandinavia and the Baltic countries. The simple two-color pattern used on the sleeves of Baltic Bodice is also very common in that region.

Baltic Bodice

"It is well to learn from the errors of others, since there is not time enough to make all of them by yourself."

—Swedish Proverb

FINISHED SIZE

37 (43½, 46)" (94 [110.5, 117] cm) chest circumference. Jacket shown measures 37" (110.5 cm). Baltic Bodice is standard fitting (see fit guidelines on page 136).

YARN (4)

Shown here: Schoolhouse Press Québéquoise (100% wool; 210 yd [192 m]/100 g): #Q99 Black (MC), 6 (6, 7) skeins; #Q71 Light Gray (CC), 2 (2, 3) skeins.

NEEDLES

Body—size 7 (4.5 mm) 24" (60-cm) circular needle (cir). Sleeves—size 5 (3.75 mm) 16" cir and set of 4 double-pointed (dpn). Cuffs—size 4 (3.5 mm) 16" (40-cm) cir. Adjust needle size if necessary to obtain the correct gauge.

NOTIONS

Safety pin; markers (m); smooth cotton scrap yarn for holders; two ⅝" (1.6 cm) buttons.

GAUGE

16 stitches and 36 rows = 4" (10 cm) in garter st using largest needle; 20 stitches and 24 rnds = 4" (10 cm) in two-color knitting pattern from Sleeve chart using middle-size needles.

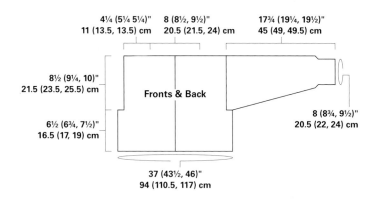

4¼ (5¼ 5¼)"
11 (13.5, 13.5) cm

8 (8½, 9½)"
20.5 (21.5, 24) cm

17¾ (19¼, 19½)"
45 (49, 49.5) cm

8½ (9¼, 10)"
21.5 (23.5, 25.5) cm

Fronts & Back

8 (8¾, 9½)"
20.5 (22, 24) cm

6½ (6¾, 7½)"
16.5 (17, 19) cm

37 (43½, 46)"
94 (110.5, 117) cm

Techniques

Chart reading (page 139), two-color knitting (page 140), three-needle bind-off (page 138), pick up by knitting (page 137).

Notes

» The lower body is worked in garter stitch in one piece to the armholes, then the back and fronts are divided and worked separately to the shoulders.

» Place a safety pin on the RS of the garter st fabric to distinguish it from the WS.

LOWER BODY

With MC and 24" (60-cm) cir in largest size, CO 148 (174, 184) sts. **Next row:** (RS) K37 (44, 46) for right front, pm for right side, k74 (86, 92) for back, pm for left side, k37 (44, 46) for left front. Work even in garter stitch (knit all sts every row) until piece measures 6½ (6¾, 7½)" (16.5 [17, 19] cm), ending with a RS row.

Reserve Underarms and Fronts

Next row: (WS) Knit to 4 (5, 6) sts past the first marker (m), place the last 8 (10, 12) sts worked on holder for left armhole, leaving m in place to identify the center of these sts later, knit to 4 (5, 6) sts past the second m, place the last 8 (10, 12) sts worked (including m) on holder for right armhole, knit to end—33 (39, 40) sts each for right and left fronts; 66 (76, 80) sts for back. Break yarn. Place both fronts on holders.

BACK

Rejoin MC to 66 (76, 80) back sts on needle with RS facing. Continue in garter st until piece measures 8½ (9¼, 10)" (21.5 [23.5, 25.5] cm) above underarm, ending with a RS row. Place sts on holder.

LEFT FRONT

Place 33 (39, 40) left front sts on the needle and rejoin MC with RS facing at armhole edge. Continue in garter st until piece measures 8½ (9¼, 10)" (21.5 [23.5, 25.5] cm) above underarm, ending with a RS row. Place sts on holder.

RIGHT FRONT

Place 33 (39, 40) left front sts on the needle and rejoin MC with RS facing at neck edge. Complete as for left front.

JOIN SHOULDERS

With WS of pieces touching and RS facing outward, join 17 (21, 21) front and back shoulder sts using the three-needle bind-off method—16 (18, 19) sts rem on holders for each front; 32 (34, 38) sts rem on holder for center back neck. The bind-off ridge will form a decorative ridge on the outside of the fabric. BO rem sts for each front.

SLEEVES

Note: Stitches for the sleeves are picked up around the armhole, and the sleeves are worked circularly down to the garter stitch cuff in two-color stranded stockinette. With MC and middle-size 16" (40-cm) cir, beg at m in center of held underarm sts k4 (5, 6) from holder, pick up by knitting 40 (42, 44) sts along armhole edge to shoulder join, then 40 (42, 44) sts along armhole edge to underarm, k4 (5, 6) rem held underarm sts—88 (94, 100) sts. Join for working in the rnd, and pm for beg of rnd. Purl 1 rnd.

Begin Color Pattern

Note: The first st of each rnd is always worked with MC. Work Rnds 1–8 of sleeve chart. **Dec rnd:** K1, k2tog in color to maintain patt, work in patt to last 2 sts, ssk in color to maintain patt—2 sts dec'd. Continue in established patt, and rep the dec rnd every 4th rnd 5 more times—76 (82, 88) sts; 29 patt rnds completed. Work even until 64 (72, 72) patt rnds (8 [9, 9] full patt reps) have been completed. Work 24 more rnds (3 patt reps) in patt, rep the dec rnd every 4th rnd 6 more times, changing to middle-size dpn when there are too few sts to work with the cir—64 (70, 76) sts. Work Rnd 1 once more—89 (97, 97) patt rnds total. **Next rnd:** With MC, k2tog 32 (35, 38) times—32 (35, 38) sts; piece measures about 15 (16¼, 16¼)" (38 [41.5, 41.5] cm) from pick-up rnd.

Sleeve

	knit with MC
	knit with CC
	pattern repeat

CUFF

Note: Cuff is worked flat in garter stitch using circular needle to accommodate the transition from working circularly to flat. Change to smallest-size needle and work in garter st back and forth in rows for 2¾ (3, 3¼)" (7 [7.5, 8.5] cm), ending with a RS row—piece measures about 17¾ (19¼, 19½)" (45 [49, 49.5] cm) from pick-up rnd. BO all sts as if to knit on the WS. Sew sides of cuff together.

FINISHING
Back Collar

Place 32 (34, 38) held back neck sts on largest cir. Join MC with WS facing and knit 8 (8, 10) rows. BO all sts loosely as if to knit on the WS.

At each side of neck, sew selvedge of back collar to the first 4 (4, 5) bound-off sts along top edge of each front. Turn back lapels and tack in place by sewing a button through both layers in the corner of each lapel as shown.

Wabi Sabi is a Japanese concept for the beauty of simplicity, of the useful, and of the worn. It is a state of mind in which one recognizes the truth that everything is just fine as it is. Based on traditional Japanese country garments made of recycled clothing, this jacket expresses the Wabi Sabi concept of understated elegance.

Wabi Sabi

"If you look up, there are no limits."

—Japanese proverb

FINISHED SIZE
45½ (49½, 53)" (115.5 [125.5, 134.5] cm) chest circumference. Jacket shown measures 49½" (125.5 cm). Wabi Sabi is loose fitting (see fit guidelines on page 136).

YARN (3)
Diakeito RU Diarufran (100% wool; 161 yd [147 m]/40 g): #215 Multicolor (MC), 6 (7, 8) balls. Elsebeth Lavold Silky Wool (65% wool, 35% silk; 191 yd [175 m]/50 g): #33 Deep Charcoal (CC), 4 (4, 5) skeins.

NEEDLES
Back and front panels—size 8 (5 mm) straight needles. Side panels and front border—size 7 (4.5 cm) 24" (60-cm) circular (cir). Sleeves and front border facing—size 5 (3.75 mm) 24" and 16" (60- and 40-cm) cir, and set of

4 double-pointed (dpn). Adjust needle size if necessary to obtain the correct gauge.

NOTIONS
Safety pin; markers (m); smooth cotton scrap yarn for holders.

GAUGE
20 stitches and 38 rows = 4" (10 cm) in garter st using MC and largest needles; 20 stitches and 38 rows = 4" (10 cm) in garter st using CC and middle-size needles; 22 stitches and 30 rows = 4" (10 cm) in stockinette using CC and smallest needles.

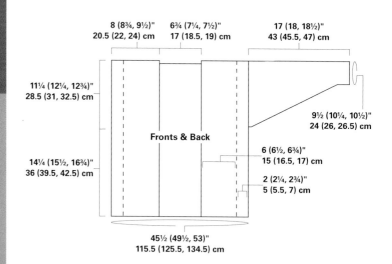

Techniques

Three-needle bind-off (page 138), pick up by knitting (page 137).

Note

» The front and back panels are worked first and joined at the shoulders. Stitches for the side panels are picked up along the edges of the fronts and back, knit outward, and then joined at the side seams. The sleeves are worked from armhole to cuff using the unjoined side panel stitches above the side seams. After joining the two halves of the jacket at the center back, a hemmed front band is worked.

Diagram labels:

8 (8¾, 9½)"
20.5 (22, 24) cm

6¾ (7¼, 7½)"
17 (18.5, 19) cm

17 (18, 18½)"
43 (45.5, 47) cm

11¼ (12¼, 12¾)"
28.5 (31, 32.5) cm

9½ (10¼, 10½)"
24 (26, 26.5) cm

Fronts & Back

6 (6½, 6¾)"
15 (16.5, 17) cm

14¼ (15½, 16¾)"
36 (39.5, 42.5) cm

2 (2¼, 2¾)"
5 (5.5, 7) cm

45½ (49½, 53)"
115.5 (125.5, 134.5) cm

RIGHT BACK PANEL

With MC and largest-size needles, CO 47 (50, 53) sts. Place a safety pin on the RS (first row) of the fabric to distinguish it from the WS. Work in garter st (knit all sts every row) for 240 (260, 276) rows (120 [130, 138] garter ridges), ending with a WS row.

Shape Back Neck

Next row: (RS) Knit to last 17 (18, 19) sts and place these sts on a holder—30 (32, 34) sts rem for right back shoulder. Turn, and knit 3 more rows—piece measures about 25½ (27¾, 29½)" (65 [70.5, 75.5] cm) from CO. Place sts on holder.

LEFT BACK PANEL

Work as for right back panel for 240 (260, 276) rows (120 [130, 138] garter ridges), ending with a WS row. Break yarn.

Shape Back Neck

Next row: (RS) With RS facing, place first 17 (18, 19) sts of row on holder. Rejoin MC to beg of rem 30 (32, 34) sts for left back shoulder, and knit 4 rows—piece measures 25½ (27¾, 29½)" (65 [70.5, 75.5] cm) from CO. Place sts on holder.

FRONT PANELS (MAKE 2)

With MC and largest-size needles, CO 30 (32, 34) sts. Place a safety pin on the RS (first row) of the fabric to distinguish it from the WS. Work in garter st for 244 (264, 280) rows (122 [132, 140] garter ridges), ending with a WS row—piece measures about 25½ (27¾, 29½)" (65 [70.5, 75.5] cm) from CO. Place sts on holder. Make a second front panel the same as the first.

JOIN SHOULDERS

With WS of pieces touching and RS facing outward, with MC join 30 (32, 34) front and back shoulder sts using the three-needle bind-off method—17 (18, 19) sts each on 2 separate holders for center back neck. The bind-off ridge will form a decorative welt on the outside of the garment.

RIGHT SIDE PANEL

With CC and middle-size 24" (60-cm) cir, beg at lower edge of right back panel pick up by knitting 122 (132, 140) sts along side selvedge of right back to shoulder join (1 st for every garter ridge), then 122 (132, 140) sts along side selvedge of right front to lower edge of right front—244 (264, 280) sts. Work striped garter st in the foll colors, ending with a RS row: 4 rows CC, 2 rows MC, 8 (10, 12) rows CC, 2 rows MC, 2 (4, 6) rows CC—18 (22, 26) total rows; piece measures about 2 (2¼, 2¾)" (5 [5.5, 7] cm) from pick-up row.

Join Side Seam

Fold piece in half with WS tog and RS facing outward. Beg at lower edge of garment and using MC, join the first and last 68 (74, 80) sts of side panel tog using the three-needle bind-off method—108 (116, 120) sts rem for right armhole. The bind-off ridge will form a decorative welt on the outside of the garment. Place sts on holder for right sleeve.

LEFT SIDE PANEL

With CC and middle-size 24" (60-cm) cir, beg at lower edge of left front panel pick up by knitting 122 (132, 140) sts along side selvedge of left front to shoulder join (1 st for every garter ridge), then 122 (132, 140) sts along side selvedge of left back to lower edge of left back—244 (264, 280) sts. Work 18 (22, 26) rows in striped garter st as for right side panel—piece measures about 2 (2¼, 2¾)" (5 [5.5, 7] cm) from pick-up row.

Join Side Seam

Work as for right side seam—108 (116, 120) sts rem for left armhole. Place sts on holder for left sleeve.

SLEEVES

Note: Sleeve shaping is worked with vertical double decrease centered on the first stitch of the round; reposition the safety pin marking this stitch every few rounds as necessary to maintain the decrease in its proper place. Place 108 (116, 120) sleeve sts on smallest-size 16" (40-cm) cir. Join for working in the rnd, and place a safety pin in the first st of the rnd. With CC, knit 3 rnds. **Dec rnd:** Knit to 1 st before marked st, sl 2 sts tog kwise (the last st of rnd with the marked st), k1, pass 2 slipped sts over—2 sts dec'd; vertical double dec st is now the first (marked) st of the next rnd. Rep the dec rnd every 4th rnd 27 (29, 30) more times, changing to smallest-size dpn when there are too few sts to fit comfortably around the cir—52 (56, 58) sts. Knit 15 rnds—piece measures about 17 (18, 18½)" (43 [45.5, 47] cm) from last row of side panel. BO all sts, and allow bound-off edge of cuff to roll up naturally to the RS. Tack rolled cuff lightly in place at 1 or 2 points.

FINISHING

Join at Center Back

With CC and middle-size 24" (60-cm) cir, with RS facing pick up by knitting 120 (130, 138) sts along right center back selvedge (1 st for every garter ridge). With CC and smallest 24" (60-cm) cir, with RS facing pick up by knitting 120 (130, 138) sts along left center back selvedge. Hold both cir tog with WS of pieces touching and RS facing outward. With CC and working with largest-size needle, join center back sts using the three-needle bind-off method. The bind-off ridge will form a decorative welt on the outside of the garment.

Front Border

Using CC and middle-size 24" (60 cm) cir, with RS facing and beg at lower edge of right front, pick up by knitting 122 (132, 140) sts along right front to shoulder join (1 st for every garter ridge), pick up 1 st from back neck shaping, k34 (36, 38) held back neck sts, pick up 1 st from back neck shaping, pick up 122 (132, 140) along left front from shoulder join to lower edge of left front—280 (302, 320) sts. Work in striped garter st in the foll colors, ending with a RS row: 4 rows CC, 2 rows MC, 8 (10, 12) rows CC, 2 rows MC, 2 (4, 6) rows CC, 2 rows MC, 4 rows CC—24 (28, 32) total rows from pick-up row; piece measures about 2½ (3, 3¼)" (6.5 [7.5, 8.5] cm) from pick-up row.

Front Border Facing

Change to smallest 24" (60-cm) cir. With CC, knit 1 WS row for turning ridge. Work 21 (23, 25) rows St st, beg and ending with a RS row. Fold facing to WS of garment along turning ridge, and tack live sts to inside of garment along front border pick-up row, taking care to sew through each st to secure.

The color pattern of Bergen is a variation of a traditional Norwegian "Fana" cardigan. The largest borough in the city of Bergen, Fana has long been a center of Norwegian life. In the nineteenth century, the Fana Sweater was worn close to the body under a vest. It emerged in WW II as a cardigan jacket, worn as a symbol of Norwegian solidarity.

Bergen

"It takes an endless amount of history to make even a little tradition."

—Henry James

FINISHED SIZE

Size A: 38½" (98 cm) chest circumference
Size B: 41¼" (105 cm) chest circumference
Size C: 44½" (113 cm) chest circumference
Size D: 49" (124.5 cm) chest circumference

Jacket shown measures 44½" (113 cm). Bergen is standard fitting (see fit guidelines on page 136).

YARN 3

Shown in: Berroco Ultra Alpaca (50% alpaca, 50% wool; 215 yd [197 m]/100 g): #6289 Charcoal Mix (MC), 4 (4, 4, 5) skeins; #6206 Light Gray (CC1), 3 (3, 3, 4) skeins; #6245 Pitch Black (CC2), 1 skein.

NEEDLES

Size A: Body and sleeves—size 4 (3.5 mm) 24" and 16" (60- and 40-cm) circular needles (cir) and set of 4 double-pointed (dpn). Bottom facing, cuffs, and front and neck borders—size 2 (2.75 mm) 24" (60-cm) cir and set of 4 dpn.

Size B: Body and sleeves—size 5 (3.75 mm) 24" and 16" (60- and 40-cm) circular needles (cir) and set of 4 double-pointed (dpn). Bottom facing, cuffs, and front and neck borders—size 3 (3.25 mm) 24" (60-cm) cir and set of 4 dpn.

Size C: Body and sleeves—size 6 (4 mm) 24" and 16" (60- and 40-cm) circular needles (cir) and set of 4 double-pointed (dpn). Bottom facing, cuffs, and front and neck borders—size 4 (3.5 mm) 24" (60-cm) cir and set of 4 dpn.

Size D: Body and sleeves—size 7 (4.5 mm) 24" and 16" (60- and 40-cm) circular needles (cir) and set of 4 double-pointed (dpn). Bottom facing, cuffs, and front and neck borders—size 5 (3.75 mm) 24" (60-cm) cir and set of 4 dpn.
Adjust needle size if necessary to obtain the correct gauge.

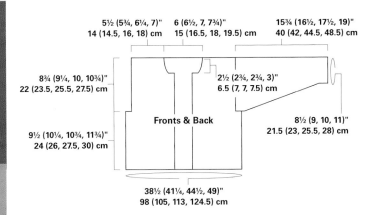

5½ (5¾, 6¼, 7)"
14 (14.5, 16, 18) cm

6 (6½, 7, 7¾)"
15 (16.5, 18, 19.5) cm

15¾ (16½, 17½, 19)"
40 (42, 44.5, 48.5) cm

8¾ (9¼, 10, 10¾)"
22 (23.5, 25.5, 27.5) cm

2½ (2¾, 2¾, 3)"
6.5 (7, 7, 7.5) cm

Fronts & Back

8½ (9, 10, 11)"
21.5 (23, 25.5, 28) cm

9½ (10¼, 10¾, 11¾)"
24 (26, 27.5, 30) cm

38½ (41¼, 44½, 49)"
98 (105, 113, 124.5) cm

NOTIONS

Markers (m); smooth cotton scrap yarn for holders; four ⅝" (1.6 cm) buttons (decorative); 2 sets of hook-and-eye (round eye) closures.

GAUGE

Size A: 26 stitches and 32 rows = 4" (10 cm) in two-color stockinette using larger needles.

Size B: 24 stitches and 30 rows = 4" (10 cm) in two-color stockinette using larger needles.

Size C: 22 stitches and 28 rows = 4" (10 cm) in two-color stockinette using larger needles.

Size D: 20 stitches and 26 rows = 4" (10 cm) in two-color stockinette using larger needles.

Work your gauge swatch from the 30-st marked section of Chart 3.

LOWER BODY

Bottom Facing

With MC and smaller 24" (60-cm) needle, CO 222 sts for all sizes using the provisional cast-on method. Working back and forth in rows, work in St st (knit RS rows, purl WS rows) for 20 rows, ending with a WS row. Change to larger 24" (60-cm) cir, and purl the next RS row for turning ridge; do not turn at the end of this row.

Steek and Join

Place a marker (pm) on the right needle, then use the attached working yarn and the backward-loop method to CO 5 sts onto the right needle for center front steek, pm—227 sts. Join for working in the rnd, being sure that your sts are not twisted, by knitting the first st on the left needle; this st becomes the first st of each rnd and is also the first st of the right front, after the center front steek sts. Continuing after the joining st, k50 more sts for right front, pm for right side, k120 sts for back, pm for left side, k51 for left front, slip steek m, work 5 steek sts.

Chart 1

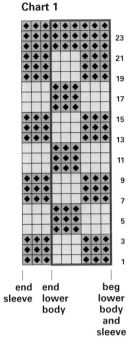

23
21
19
17
15
13
11
9
7
5
3
1

end
sleeve

end
lower
body

beg
lower
body
and
sleeve

Chart 2

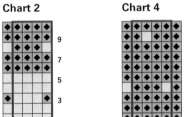

9
7
5
3
1

Chart 4

9
7
5
3
1

◆ knit with MC

knit with CC1

pattern repeat

Chart 3

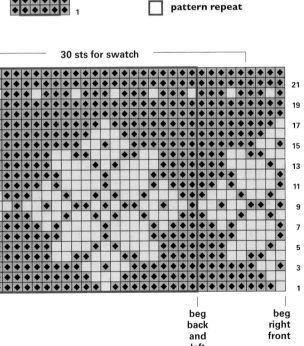

21
19
17
15
13
11
9
7
5
3
1

30 sts for swatch

end
left
front

end
back
and
right
front

beg
back
and
left
front

beg
right
front

Begin Color Patterns

Work Rnd 1 of Chart 1 over first 222 sts, beg and ending where indicated for lower body, slip steek m, work 5 steek sts. Continuing as established, work Rnds 2–24 of Chart 1, dec 1 back st in Rnd 24—226 sts total; 221 lower body sts; 5 steek sts. Change to Chart 2, rep Rnds 1–10 a total of 5 times, then work Rnds 1 and 2 once more—76 chart rnds above turning ridge; piece measures about 9½ (10¼, 10¾, 11¾)" (24 [26, 27.5, 30] cm) from turning ridge.

Steek Armholes and Reserve Underarms

Next rnd: (Rnd 3 of chart) Work in established patt to 6 sts before right side m, *place the next 11 sts (including marker), on holder, pm, CO 5 sts onto right needle for steek, pm;* work in patt to 5 sts before left side m; rep from * to * once more for left armhole steek, work in patt to end—214 sts total; 45 sts each for right and left fronts; 109 sts for back; 5 sts in each steek at center front and both armholes. Continuing patt as established in each section, work Rnds 4–10 of Chart 2 once, then work Rnds 1–9 once more. **Next rnd:** (Rnd 10 of chart) Work in patt, inc 1 st in each front —216 sts; 46 sts each for right and left fronts; 109 sts for back; 5 sts in each steek at center front and both armholes. Work Rnd 1 from Chart 3 as foll: For right front, work 46 sts beg and ending where indicated; work 5 armhole steek sts; for back, work 36-st patt rep 3 times, then work 1 st after patt rep box; work 5 armhole steek sts; for left front, work 46 sts beg and ending where indicated; work 5 center front steek sts. Work Rnds 2–18 of chart. **Next rnd:** (Rnd 19 of chart) Work in patt, dec 1 st at end of right front sts, and dec 1 st at beg of left front sts—214 sts total; 45 sts each for right and left fronts. Work Rnds 20–22 of chart. Change to Chart 2, and beg and ending chart separately for each front and the back, work Rnds 1–10—126 chart rnds total above turning ridge; 50 rnds above start of armhole steeks; piece measures about 6¼ (6½, 7¼, 7¾)" (16 [16.5, 18.5, 19.5] cm) above underarms. Break yarns.

Steek Front Neck

Place 5 center front steek sts and 7 sts on each side of them on holder. Pm on right needle, use CC1 to CO 5 neck steek sts onto right needle above held center front sts, pm—200 sts total; 38 sts each rem for right and left fronts; 109 sts for back; 5 sts each for steeks at neck and both armholes. Join for working in the rnd again by knitting the first st on the left needle; this st becomes the first st of each rnd and is also the first st of the right front, after the neck steek sts. Knit to end of rnd—counts as Rnd 1 of Chart 2.

Neck Shaping

Continue in patt from Chart 2, working neck shaping on each side of neck steek as foll:

Rnd 2: (dec rnd) Work 1 st in patt, ssk, knit to 3 sts before neck steek, k2tog, k1—1 st dec'd from each front at neck edge.

Rnds 3 and 5: Work even in patt.

Rnds 4 and 6: (dec rnds) Continuing in patt, rep shaping of Rnd 2—35 sts each for right and left fronts after completing Rnd 6.

Continuing in established patt, work Rnds 7–10 of chart once, then work Rnds 1–10 once more—146 chart rnds total above turning ridge; 70 rnds above start of armhole steeks; 20 rnds above start of neck steek; piece measures 8¾ (9¼, 10, 10¾)" (22 [23.5, 25.5, 27.5] cm) above underarms, and 2½ (2¾, 2¾, 3)" (6.5 [7, 7, 7.5] cm) above start of neck shaping. Place sts on holder.

STITCHING AND CUTTING

Machine stitch and cut the steeks for center front, neck, and both armholes.

JOIN SHOULDERS

With RS of pieces touching and WS facing outward, join 35 front and back shoulder sts using the three-needle bind-off method—39 sts rem on holder for center back neck.

SLEEVES

Note: Sleeves are worked in the round from cuffs upward, then attached to the body by binding off the live sleeve stitches together with stitches picked up around the armhole opening using the three-needle bind-off method. With MC and smaller dpn, CO 55 sts. Working back and forth in rows, work in garter st (knit all sts every row) for 10 rows. Change to CC2 and work 4 rows in garter st, ending with a WS row. Change to MC and larger dpn. Join for working in the rnd, and pm for beg of rnd. With CC1, knit 3 rnds, inc 11 sts evenly spaced in last rnd—66 sts; these 3 rnds count as Rnds 1–3 of Chart 4. Work Rnd 4 of chart.

Sleeve Shaping

Notes: Work the first stitch of every round with MC throughout the sleeve shaping, and incorporate new stitches into the established pattern. **Next rnd:** (inc rnd) Using the backward-loop method for all incs, k1, inc 1, work in patt to end, inc 1—2 sts inc'd. Continue in established patt, rep the inc rnd every 5th rnd 19 more times, changing to larger 16" (40-cm) cir when there are too many sts to fit on the dpn, and ending with Rnd 10 of chart—106 sts; 100 chart rnds above garter st cuff. With MC, knit 3 rnds. Work Rnd 13 from Chart 1 as foll: K1 with MC, work 105 sts in patt from chart, beg and ending where indicated for sleeve. Working first st of rnd in MC as established, work Rnds 14–24 of chart—115 rnds completed above garter st cuff; piece measures about 15¾ (16½, 17½, 19)" (40 [42, 44.5, 49.5] cm) from CO. Place sts on holder or leave on the needle if attaching to body immediately.

Set up Armholes and Attach Sleeves

Note: Leave underarm holder strings in place until after the underarm sts have been attached, then remove holders. With larger 24" (60-cm) cir and RS facing, using MC and beg at m for right armhole steek, k5 sts from holder, pick up by knitting 47 sts along armhole edge to shoulder join, pick up 1 st in join, then 47 sts along armhole edge to underarm, k6 rem held underarm sts—106 sts. With RS of pieces touching and WS facing outward, beg at underarm m, join 106 live sts at top of sleeve to 106 sts picked up around armhole using the three-needle bind-off method. Join left sleeve in the same manner, except that the left armhole pick-up begins with k6 from holder, and ends with k5 from holder.

FINISHING

Bottom Hem

Fold bottom facing to WS along turning ridge. Carefully re-moving provisional cast-on as you work, sew live CO sts of facing to garment on WS. **Tip:** To keep the hem flexible and invisible, be careful not to pull the hem stitching too tight.

Right Front Border

With CC2 and smaller 24" (60-cm) cir, with RS facing and beg at right front turning ridge, pick up by knitting 85 sts along right front to start of neck shaping. Work 3 rows in garter st, beg and ending with a WS row. Change to MC, and work 20 rows in garter st, ending with as WS row—12 garter ridges total. Work in St st for 8 rows, ending with a WS row. BO loosely as if to knit, and allow bound-off front edge to roll naturally to the RS.

Left Front Border

With CC2 and smaller 24" (60-cm) cir, with RS facing and beg at left front neck shaping, pick up by knitting 85 sts along left front to turning ridge. Complete as for right front border.

Neck Border

With CC2 and smaller 24" (60- or 40-cm) cir, RS facing and beg at right front edge, pick up by knitting 2 sts from selvedge of rolled edge picking up through all layers of roll, then 12 sts across rest of front border selvedge, k7 from right front neck holder, pick up by knitting 13 sts along shaped right neck edge to shoulder join, 1 st in shoulder, k39 from back neck holder, pick up by knitting 1 st in shoulder, 13 sts along shaped left neck edge to holder, k7 from left front neck holder, pick up by knitting 12 sts across front border selvedge to rolled edge, and 2 sts through all layers of roll—109 sts. Work 3 rows garter st. Change to MC, and work 11 rows in garter st, ending with a RS row. BO loosely as if to knit.

Buttons and Hooks

Sew 2 buttons to each front border as shown in photo-graph, with the upper button right below the neck border, and the lower button even with the second light-colored stripe below Chart 3. Sew hook-and-eye closures to WS of each front border, aligned with button locations and positioned so that the rolled edges will conceal the hooks and eyes when the garment is hooked closed.

The past becomes a texture, an ambience to our present.

—Paul Scott, author of the Raj Quartet

Texture

The widely varied textures that can be created with knitting make it one of the most versatile of textiles. Here you will find jackets created with cables, knit-purl patterns, slip stitches and even knitted lace. From the most traditional Aran cardigan to the Japanese-style *hanten*, texture gives knitting its "feel."

The Bloomsbury area of London, near the British Museum, was home in the early twentieth century to a group of writers who came to be known as the Bloomsbury group. These were young, modern thinkers who sought a cultural renaissance as the Victorian influences passed away. Bloomsbury Jacket is a tribute to this talented circle.

Bloomsbury Jacket

"Walk on a rainbow trail; walk on a trail of song, and all about you will be beauty."

—Virginia Woolf

FINISHED SIZE

Size A: 40½" (103 cm) chest circumference

Size B: 44" (112 cm) chest circumference

Size C: 48" (122 cm) chest circumference

Jacket shown measures 44" (112 cm). Bloomsbury is standard fitting (see fit guidelines on page 136).

YARN 〔4〕

Shown here: Jo Sharp Silkroad Aran (85% wool, 10% silk, 5% cashmere; 93 yds (85 m)/50 g): #106 Batik, 18 balls for all sizes.

NEEDLES

Size A: Body and sleeves—size 7 (4.5 mm) 24" and 16" (60- and 40-cm) circular needles (cir). Bottom border and cuffs—size 4 (3.5 mm) 24" and 16" (60- and 40-cm) cir. Collar and front borders—size 5 (3.75 mm) 24" (60-cm) cir.

Size B: Body and sleeves—size 8 (5 mm) 24" and 16" (60- and 40-cm) circular needles (cir). Bottom border and cuffs—size 5 (3.75 mm) 24" and 16" (60- and 40-cm) cir. Collar and front borders—size 6 (4 mm) 24" (60-cm) cir.

Size C: Body and sleeves—size 9 (5.5 mm) 24" and 16" (60 and 40-cm) circular needles (cir). Bottom border and cuffs—size 6 (4 mm) 24" and 16" (60- and 40-cm) cir. Collar and front borders—size 7 (4.5 mm) 24" (60-cm) cir. Adjust needle size if necessary to obtain the correct gauge.

NOTIONS

Markers (m); smooth cotton scrap yarn for holders; cable needle (cn); five ¾" (2 cm) buttons.

Techniques

Backward-loop increase (page 137), three-needle bind-off (page 138), pick up by knitting (page 137), short rows (page 138).

Notes

» The size of the jacket is determined by the needle size—the larger sizes are made using larger needles. For this reason, doing a gauge swatch is very important!

» The lower body is worked in one piece to the armholes, then the back and fronts are divided and worked separately to the shoulders.

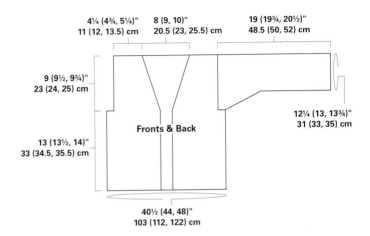

GAUGE

Size A: 17 stitches and 25 rows = 4" (10 cm) in stockinette using largest needles; 22 stitches and 25 rows = 4" (10 cm) in cable and garter pattern from Body chart using largest needles.

Size B: 16 stitches and 24 rows = 4" (10 cm) in stockinette using largest needles; 20 stitches and 24 rows = 4" (10 cm) in cable and garter pattern from Body chart using largest needles.

Size C: 15 stitches and 23 rows = 4" (10 cm) in stockinette using largest needles; 18 stitches and 23 rows = 4" (10 cm) in cable and garter pattern from Body chart using largest needles.

LOWER BODY

Bottom Border

With smallest 24" (60-cm) cir, CO 199 sts for all sizes. Work in garter st (knit all sts every row) for 10 rows, ending with a RS row—piece measures about 1½" (3.8 cm) from CO.

Body

Change to largest 24" (60-cm) cir. **Set-up row:** (WS) Using the backward-loop method for all incs, p1, k1, *p2, inc 1, p3, k5; rep from * to last 7 sts, p2, inc 1, p3, k1, p1—219 sts. Work Rows 1–8 of Body chart 8 times, then work Rows 1–6 once more—70 rows completed from chart. Work Row 7 of chart, placing markers (pm) as foll: (RS) Work 49 sts in patt for right front, pm for right side, work 121 sts in patt for back, pm for left side, work 49 sts in patt to end for left front; each m is in the center of a 6-st cable panel.

Reserve Underarms and Fronts

Next row: (WS, Row 8 of chart) Work in patt to 6 sts past the first m, place the last 12 sts worked on holder for left armhole, leaving m in place to identify the center of these sts later, work in patt to 6 sts past the second m, place the last 12 sts worked (including m) on holder for right armhole, work to end of row—43 sts each for right and left fronts; 109 sts for back; piece measures about 13 (13½, 14)" (33 [34.5, 35.5] cm) from CO. Break yarn. Place both fronts on holders.

BACK

Rejoin yarn to 109 back sts on needle with RS facing.

Row 1: (RS, Row 1 of chart) K1, ssk, work in patt to last 3 sts, k2tog, k1—2 sts dec'd.

Row 2: Work even in patt.

Rep Rows 1 and 2 seven more times, ending with Row 8 of chart—93 sts.

Rep Rows 1–8 five more times—56 rows (7 full reps) of patt completed above the underarm; piece measures 9 (9½, 9¾)" (23 [24, 25] cm) above underarm. Place sts on holder.

LEFT FRONT

Note: Armhole and neck shaping are worked at the same time. Place 43 held left front sts on largest 24" (60-cm) cir and rejoin yarn with RS facing at armhole edge. **Next row**: (RS, Row 1 of chart) K1, ssk (armhole shaping), work in patt to last 3 sts, k2tog, k1 (neck shaping), mark the last stitch in this row for start of neck shaping—2 sts dec'd total, 1 st each from armhole and neck edges. Dec 1 st at armhole edge in this manner on the next 7 RS rows, and at the same time, dec 1 st at neck edge in this manner every 4th row 10 more times—24 sts rem when all armhole and neck shaping have been completed. Work even in patt until 56 rows (7 full reps) of patt have been completed above the underarm, ending with Row 8 of patt—piece measures 9 (9½, 9¾)" (23 [24, 25] cm) above underarm. Place sts on holder.

RIGHT FRONT

Note: As for left front, armhole and neck shaping are worked at the same time. Place 43 held left front sts on largest 24" (60-cm) cir and rejoin yarn with RS facing at neck edge. **Next row**: (RS, Row 1 of chart) Mark the first stitch for start of neck shaping, k1, ssk (neck shaping), work in patt to last 3 sts, k2tog, k1 (armhole shaping)—2 sts dec'd total, 1 st each from armhole and neck edges. Dec 1 st at armhole edge in this manner on the next 7 RS rows, and at the same time, dec 1 st at neck edge in this manner every 4th row 10 more

Sleeve

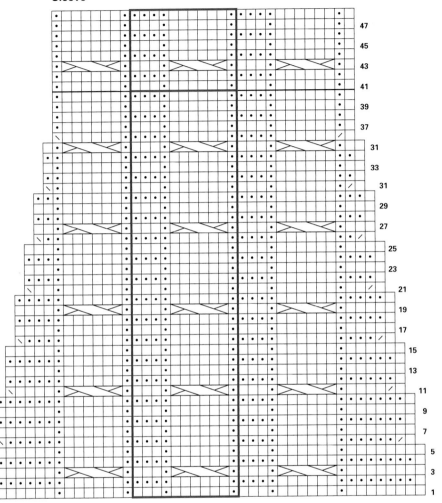

	47
	45
	43
	41
	39
	37
	31
	33
	31
	29
	27
	25
	23
	21
	19
	17
	15
	13
	11
	9
	7
	5
	3
	1

Body

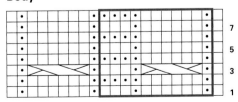

	7
	5
	3
	1

☐	**k on RS rows and all rnds; p on WS rows**
・	**p on RS rows and all rnds; k on WS rows**
╱	**k2tog**
╲	**ssk**
☐	**pattern repeat**
✕	**sl 3 sts onto cn and hold in front, k3, k3 from cn**

times—24 sts rem when all armhole and neck shaping have been completed. Work even in patt until 56 rows (7 full reps) of patt have been completed above the underarm, ending with Row 8 of patt—piece measures 9 (9½, 9¾)" (23 [24, 25] cm) above underarm. Place sts on holder.

JOIN SHOULDERS

With RS of pieces touching and WS facing outward, join 24 front and back shoulder sts using the three-needle bind-off method—45 sts rem on holder for center back neck.

SLEEVES

Notes: Stitches for the sleeves are picked up around the armhole and the sleeves are worked circularly down to the wrist. Using larger 16" (40-cm) cir, beg at marker in center of held underarm sts, k6 from holder, pick up by knitting 39 sts along armhole edge to shoulder join, then 38 sts along armhole edge to underarm, k6, rem held underarm sts—89 sts. Join for working in the rnd, and pm for beg of rnd. **Set-up rnd:** K1, p8, *k6, p5; rep from * to last 14 sts, k6, p8. Work Rnds 1–5 of Sleeve chart, reading all chart rows as RS rnds.

Sleeve Shaping

Note: Work the first st of every rnd as k1; shaping decreases will be worked on each side of this knit st. **Next rnd:** (Rnd 6 of chart) K1, k2tog, work in patt to last 2 sts, ssk—2 sts dec'd. Work Rnds 7–40 of chart once, dec as shown—75 sts rem after Rnd 36. Rep Rnds 41–48 of chart 8 more times—104 patt rnds (13 full reps of 8-rnd cable patt) have been completed; piece measures about 16¾ (17½, 18¼)" (42.5 [44.5, 46.5] cm) from pick-up rnd.

Cuff

Note: The cuff is worked circularly in garter st (knit one rnd, purl one rnd) on all sts, with 2 dec rnds for shaping.

Change to smaller 16" (40-cm) cir.

Rnd 1: *[K2, k2tog] 2 times, k5; rep from * to last 10 sts, [k2, k2tog] 2 times, k2—63 sts.

Rnd 2: Purl.

Rnd 3: Knit.

Rnds 4–10: Rep Rnds 2 and 3 three more times, then work Rnd 2 once more.

Rnd 11: *K4, k2tog; rep from * to last 3 sts, k1, k2tog—52 sts.

Rnds 12–21: Rep Rnds 2 and 3 five more times—piece measures about 19 (19¾, 20½)" (48.5 [50, 52] cm) from pick-up rnd.

BO as if to purl.

FINISHING
Collar and Front Borders

Note: The collar and front borders are knitted in one piece in garter st with short-row shaping for the collar. With mid-sized 24" (60-cm) cir and RS facing, beg at lower edge of right front pick up by knitting 50 sts up to first neck shaping m, then 38 sts from m to shoulder join, knit first 22 sts from back neck holder, k1 and mark this st for center back, knit the last 22 sts from back neck holder, pick up by knitting 38 sts from shoulder join to next neck shaping m, then 50 sts from m to lower edge of left front—221 sts.

Collar Shaping

Short-row 1: (WS) Knit to the marked center back st, knit marked st, k1, wrap next st and turn (WT).

Short-row 2: (RS) Knit to marked center st, knit marked st, k1, WT—first short-row set completed; wrapped sts are the 2nd sts on each side of marked center st.

> **Note:** If you are accustomed to working wrapped sts tog with their wraps, it is not necessary to do so in garter st; simply knit each wrapped st as you come to it.

Short-rows 3 and 4: Knit to previously wrapped st, knit wrapped st, k1, WT—second short-row set completed; wrapped sts are the 4th sts on each side of marked center st.

Short-rows 5–60: Rep Short-rows 3 and 4 twenty-eight more times, working each new wrapped st 2 sts past the previous wrapped st and 2 sts farther out from the marked center st in each set of short-rows, ending at left front neck shaping m—last wrapped st at each side is marked neck shaping st; collar measures about 5¾ (6, 6¼)" (14.5 [15, 16] cm) from pick-up row at center back neck.

Front Borders

Next 2 rows: Knit to end—all sts have been worked. Continue in garter st for 14 more rows, ending with a RS row—front bands measure about 2 (2½, 3)" (5 [6.5, 7.5] cm) from pick-up row.

Bind Off and Make Button Loops

BO off as if to knit up to left front neck shaping m, then BO as if to purl around collar to the right front neck shaping m, then BO as if to knit as foll to create 4 button loops: BO 4 sts (1 st on right needle after last BO), *[yo, pass 1st st on right needle over yo] 3 times, BO next 9 sts; rep from * 3 more times, [yo, pass 1st st on right needle over yo] 3 times, BO to end.

Sew buttons into place on left front to correspond to button loops.

Here is texture and technique enough to please any knitter, with pieces that fit together like a good puzzle. The body is a combination garter and slip-stitch pattern that is complemented with one cable panel on the sleeve, saddle shoulder, and front band. There's I-cord on the front edge and, to top it off, the jacket is put together with three-needle bind-off.

"Who in the world am I? Ah, that's the great puzzle."

—Lewis Carroll

Puzzle Me This

FINISHED SIZE
43¼ x (48½, 54)" (110 [123, 137] cm) chest circumference. Jacket shown measures 48½" (123 cm). Puzzle Me This is oversize (see fit guidelines on page 136).

YARN 4
Shown in: Harrisville New England Knitter's Highland (100% wool; about 200 yd [183 m]/100 g): #19 Blackberry, 6 (7, 8) skeins.

Needles
Size 8 (5 mm): Two 24" (60-cm) circular needles (cir).
Adjust needle size if necessary to obtain the correct gauge.

NOTIONS
Markers (m); cable needle (cn); smooth cotton scrap yarn for holders; size 10 (6 mm) needle of any kind (used for three-needle bind-off only).

GAUGE
16 stitches and 24 rows = 4" (10 cm) in stockinette; 18 stitches and 38 rows = 4" (10 cm) in Garter Slip-Stitch pattern from chart; 20-st marked center cable section of Sleeve chart measures about 3½" (9 cm) wide.

Techniques

Chart reading (page 139), slip stitches (page 141), k1f&b increase (page 137), three-needle bind-off (page 138), pick up by knitting (page 137).

Stitch Guide

Wrap Yarn Twice Around Needle:

Insert needle tip into next st as if to knit, wrap yarn twice around needle, pull both wraps through, drop old st from left needle. When slipping this stitch purlwise on the following WS row, drop one of its wraps, leaving a single elongated stitch.

Notes

» Successful construction is dependent on accurate row counts throughout. Always count your rows, using a row counter if necessary.

» Slip the first stitch of every row as if to purl with yarn in front (pwise wyf). This makes it easy to pick up stitches for attaching sleeves, saddle shoulders, and front bands and for sewing sleeve seams.

» The lower body is worked entirely in Garter Slip-Stitch pattern in one piece to the armholes, then the back and fronts are divided and worked separately in pattern to the shoulders.

» On the sleeves, the same Garter Slip-Stitch pattern is used in conjunction with a central cable panel that continues into the saddle shoulder extension at the top of each sleeve. This same cable is also used for the front bands.

» Use a needle at least two sizes larger than the main needles for the three-needle bind-off to keep it flexible.

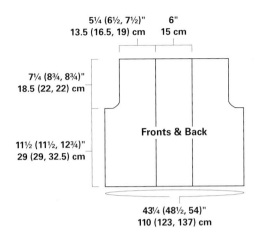

5¼ (6½, 7½)"   6"
13.5 (16.5, 19) cm   15 cm

7¼ (8¾, 8¾)"
18.5 (22, 22) cm

Fronts & Back

11½ (11½, 12¾)"
29 (29, 32.5) cm

43¼ (48½, 54)"
110 (123, 137) cm

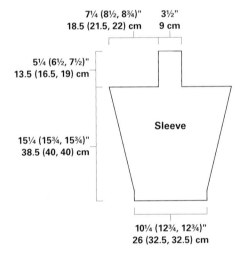

7¼ (8½, 8¾)"   3½"
18.5 (21.5, 22) cm   9 cm

5¼ (6½, 7½)"
13.5 (16.5, 19) cm

Sleeve

15¼ (15¾, 15¾)"
38.5 (40, 40) cm

10¼ (12¾, 12¾)"
26 (32.5, 32.5) cm

LOWER BODY

CO 161 (185, 209) sts. **Next row:** (WS) Sl 1 (see Notes), k33 (39, 45), place marker (pm) for left side, k93 (105, 117) for back, pm for right side, k34 (40, 46) for right front. Work in patt from Garter Slip-Stitch chart until 9 (9, 10) reps of Rows 1–12 have been completed, then work Row 1 once more—109 (109, 121) patt rows completed from chart.

Reserve Underarms and Fronts

Next row: (WS, Row 2 of chart) Work in patt to 6 sts past the first side m, place the last 13 sts worked on holder for left armhole (including m), work in patt to 7 sts past the next side m, place the last 13 sts worked (including m) on holder for right armhole, work in patt to end of right front—27 (33, 39) sts for each front; 81 (93, 105) sts for back. Break yarn. Place both fronts on holders.

Back

Rejoin yarn to 81 (93, 105) back sts on needle with RS facing. **Dec row:** (RS, Row 3 of chart) Sl 1, ssk, work in patt to last 3 sts, k2tog, k1—2 sts dec'd. Continuing in established patt, rep the dec row on the next 2 (3, 4) RS rows, ending with Row 7 (9, 11) of chart—75 (85, 95) sts rem. Work 5 (3, 1) more row(s) even to complete 10 (10, 11) full patt reps. Rep Rows 1–12 of chart 5 (6, 6) more times—15 (16, 17) full patt reps completed from beg. Place sts on holder.

RIGHT FRONT

Place 27 (33, 39) held right front sts on needle and rejoin yarn with RS facing at neck edge. **Dec row:** (RS) Work in patt to last 3 sts, k2tog, k1—1 st dec'd. Continuing in established patt, rep the dec row on the next 2 (3, 4) RS rows, ending with Row 7 (9, 11) of chart—24 (29, 34) sts rem. Continue in established patt until 15 (16, 17) full patt reps have been completed from beg. Place sts on holder.

Sleeve

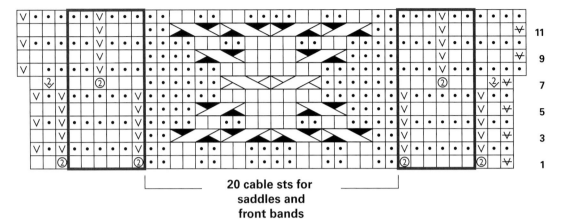

20 cable sts for
saddles and
front bands

Garter Slip Stitch

		k on RS; p on WS
•		p on RS; k on WS
V		sl 1 pwise wyb on RS; sl 1 pwise wyf on WS
⊬		sl 1 pwise wyf on RS
②		wrap yarn twice around needle (see Stitch Guide)
↓		k1f&b
		pattern repeat

sl 2 sts onto cn and hold in back,
k2, k2 from cn

sl 2 sts onto cn and hold in front,
k2, k2 from cn

sl 2 sts onto cn and hold in back,
k2, p2 from cn

sl 2 sts onto cn and hold in front,
p2, k2 from cn

LEFT FRONT

Place 27 (33, 39) held left front sts on needle and rejoin yarn with RS facing at armhole edge. **Dec row:** (RS) K1, ssk, work in patt to end—1 st dec'd. Continuing in established patt, rep the dec row on the next 2 (3, 4) RS rows, ending with Row 7 (9, 11) of chart—24 (29, 34) sts rem. Continue in established patt until 15 (16, 17) full patt reps have been completed from beg. Place sts on holder.

SLEEVES

Note: The sleeves are worked from the cuff to the shoulders, with the central cable continuing into saddle shoulder extensions. CO 50 (62, 62) sts. **Next row:** (WS) Sl 1, k14 (20, 20), pm, [k2, p2] 2 times, k4, [p2, k2] 2 times, pm, k15 (21, 21). Work Row 1 of Sleeve chart as foll: Work 3 sts before first patt rep box once, work first 6-st patt rep 2 (3, 3) times, work center 20 sts in cable patt, work second 6-st patt rep 2 (3, 3) times, work 3 sts after patt rep box once. Work Rows 2–6 of Sleeve chart. **Inc row:** (RS) Sl 1, k1f&b, work in patt to last 2 sts, k1f&b, k1—2 sts inc'd. Continuing in established patt, rep inc row every 8th row 17 (16, 16) times, then every 6th row 0 (0, 2) times, and incorporate the new sts into established Garter Slip-Stitch patt at each side—86 (96, 100) sts total; 33 (38, 40) sts in Garter Slip Stitch on each side of center 20 cable sts. Work even in patt until 144 (150, 150) patt rows total have been completed from beg (12 [12½, 12½] patt reps). Place 33 (38, 40) sts on each side of 20-st center cable panel on separate holders. Continue in established patt on cable sts for 30 (38, 44) more rows for saddle shoulder, ending with a WS row—174 (188, 194) patt rows total from beg.

Note: Cable sts without surrounding sts in Garter Slip Stitch have a row gauge of about 23 rows = 4" (10 cm). Saddle extension measures about 5¼ (6½, 7½)" (13.5 [16.5, 19] cm) from where sts were put on holders at each side. Place sts on holder.

FINISHING

Attach Left Sleeve

Beg at left back shoulder line, pick up by knitting 27 (32, 34) sts along left back armhole edge (about 3 sts for every 4 slipped edge sts), k13 from underarm holder dec 1 st in center of underarm, pick up by knitting 27 (32, 34) sts along left front armhole edge to shoulder line—66 (76, 80) sts. With RS facing, place 33 (38, 40) sleeve sts before the saddle extension on empty needle. Hold needles tog with WS of pieces touching and RS facing outward. Using larger needle for binding off and working from shoulder line to base of armhole, join 33 (38, 40) live sleeve sts to first 33 (38, 40) picked-up sts of armhole using the three-needle bind-off method; the bind-off ridge will form a decorative welt on the outside of the garment. With RS still facing, place rem 33 (38, 40) held sleeve sts after cable on empty needle. Hold needles tog with WS of pieces touching and RS facing outward, and continue the three-needle bind-off from base of armhole to shoulder line to attach rem live sleeve sts to rem picked-up armhole sts. Sew sleeve seam from underarm to CO edge.

Attach Right Sleeve

Beg at right front shoulder line, pick up by knitting 66 (76, 80) sts around right armhole as for left armhole. Attach right sleeve as for left sleeve. Sew sleeve seam from underarm to CO edge.

Attach Left Saddle Shoulder

With RS facing and beg at bound-off end of saddle extension, pick up by knitting 24 (29, 34) sts along selvedge of saddle extension. Place 24 (29, 34) held sts of left front on empty needle. Hold needles tog with WS of pieces touching and RS facing outward. Using larger needle for binding off and working from armhole edge to neck edge, join live front sts to picked-up saddle sts using the three-needle bind-off method. With RS facing and beg at corner

at base of saddle extension, pick up by knitting 24 (29, 34) sts along selvedge of saddle extension. Place 24 (29, 34) held sts of left back on empty needle. Hold needles tog with WS of pieces touching and RS facing outward. Using larger needle for binding off and working from neck edge to armhole edge so bind-off ridges will look the same on both sides, join live back sts to picked-up saddle sts using the three-needle bind-off method.

Attach Right Saddle Shoulder

With RS facing and beg at corner at base of saddle extension, pick up by knitting 24 (29, 34) sts along selvedge of saddle extension. Place 24 (29, 34) held sts of right front on empty needle. Hold needles tog with WS of pieces touching and RS facing outward. Using larger needle for binding off and working from neck edge to armhole edge, join live front sts to picked-up saddle sts using the three-needle bind-off method. With RS facing and beg at bound-off end of saddle extension, pick up by knitting 24 (29, 34) sts along selvedge of saddle extension. Place 24 (29, 34) held sts of right back on second cir—27 sts rem on holder for center back neck. Hold needles tog with WS of pieces touching and RS facing outward. Using larger needle for binding off and working from armhole edge to neck edge so bind-off ridges will look the same on both sides, join live back sts to picked-up saddle sts using the three-needle bind-off method.

Front Bands

Note: The front bands are worked separately from lower edge to the middle of the back neck in cable patt with I-cord edging. The bands are joined to the body using a three-needle bind-off, and then joined to each other at center back neck as a continuation of that bind-off.

Right Front Band

CO 24 sts. **Set-up row:** (WS) Sl 1 pwise wyf, k6, p8, k6, sl 3 pwise wyf. **Next row:** (RS) Bring yarn up behind work and knit first 3 sts for I-cord at neck edge, work Row 7 of

marked cable panel from Sleeve chart over next 20 sts, k1.
Next row: (WS) Sl 1 pwise wyf, work Row 8 of marked cable panel over next 20 sts, sl 3 pwise wyf for I-cord at neck edge. For remainder of band, work 3 sts for I-cord at neck edge as k3 on RS rows and sl 3 pwise wyf on WS rows; and work single st at other selvedge as k1 on RS rows and sl 1 pwise wyf on WS rows. Continuing all patts as established, work Rows 9–12 of cable patt once, rep Rows 1–12 of cable patt 14 (15, 16) times, then work Rows 1–10 (1–6, 1–2) once more—184 (192, 200) rows total in cable patt. Place sts on holder.

Left Front Band

CO 24 sts. Set-up row: (WS) P3, k6, p8, k6, p1.
Next row: (RS) Sl 1 pwise wyf, work Row 7 of marked cable panel from Sleeve chart over next 20 sts, sl 3 pwise with yarn in back (wyb). **Next row:** (WS) Bring yarn up across front of work and purl first 3 sts for I-cord at neck edge, work Row 8 of marked cable panel over next 20 sts, p1. For remainder of band, work 3 sts for I-cord at neck edge as sl 3 pwise wyb on RS rows and p3 on WS rows; and work single st at other selvedge as sl 1 pwise wyf on RS rows and p1 on WS rows. Continuing all patts as established, work Rows 9–12 of cable patt once, rep Rows 1–12 of cable patt 14 (15, 16) times, then work Rows 1–10 (1–6, 1–2) once more—184 (192, 200) rows total in cable patt. Place sts on holder.

Attach Right Front Band

With RS facing and beg at CO edge of right front, pick up by knitting 45 (48, 51) sts from lower edge of right front to front saddle join (1 st for every other slipped front edge st), work k2tog 10 times across 20 held right saddle sts to dec them to 10 sts, work k2tog 6 times across first 12 held back neck sts dec them to 6 sts—61 (64, 67) sts; 15 sts rem on holder for center back neck. With empty needle and RS facing, beg at last row of band pick up by knitting 61 (64, 67) sts along slipped st selvedge of right front band

(about 2 sts for every 3 slipped edge sts). Hold needles tog with WS of pieces touching and RS facing outward. Using larger needle for binding off and working from CO edge of body to center back neck, join sts using the three-needle bind-off method.

Attach Left Front Band

With RS facing, leave first 3 held back neck sts on holder at center back neck. With RS facing and beg at 4th held back neck st, work k2tog 6 times across rem 12 back neck sts dec them to 6 sts, work k2tog 10 times across 20 held left saddle sts dec them to 10 sts, pick up by knitting 45 (48, 51) sts from saddle join to lower edge of left front (1 st for every other slipped front edge st)—61 (64, 67) sts. With empty needle and RS facing, beg at CO edge of band, pick up by knitting 61 (64, 67) sts along slipped st selvedge of left front band (about 2 sts for every 3 slipped edge sts). Hold needles tog with WS of pieces touching and RS facing outward. Using larger needle for binding off and working from center back neck to lower edge of body, join sts using the three-needle bind-off method.

Back Neck Seam

Place 24 sts for each front band and 1 back neck st from each side of center back st on separate needles—25 sts on each needle; 1 center back st rem on holder. Hold needles with RS tog and WS facing outward; the ridge for this join will be on the inside of the garment. Beg at I-cord edge and working toward neck edge, use the three-needle bind-off method to join live sts on needles tog, then pass final BO st over rem center back neck st, and fasten off last st.

The early twentieth century was a period of expansive change. As the Victorian age gave way to "modern" Edwardian influences, women loosened their corsets, raised their consciousness, and sought the vote. Clothing softened and comfortable knitted jackets became favorites for daywear, perfect for croquet or for taking tea on a cool afternoon.

Edwardian Day Coat

"Though always well bred, there often lurked a flash of mischief in her eyes."

—Susan E. Meyer describing the Gibson Girl in her book *America's Great Illustrators*

FINISHED SIZE

Size A: 40" (101.5 cm) chest circumference
Size B: 43" (109 cm) chest circumference
Size C: 46¼" (117.5 cm) chest circumference
Size D: 50¼" (127.5 cm) chest circumference

Jacket shown measures 46¼" (117.5 cm). Edwardian Day Coat is loose fitting (see fit guidelines on page 136).

YARN 4

Shown here: Ella Rae Classic (100% wool; 219 yd [200 m]/100 g): #13 Dusty Teal, 9 balls for all sizes.

NEEDLES

Size A: Body and sleeves—size 5 (3.75 mm) 24" (60-cm) circular (cir) and set of 4 double-pointed (dpn). Bottom border, cuffs, front bands, and collar—size 2 (2.75 mm) 24" (60-cm) circular (cir) and set of 4 double-pointed (dpn).

Size B: Body and sleeves—size 6 (4 mm) 24" (60-cm) circular (cir) and set of 4 double-pointed (dpn). Bottom border, cuffs, front bands, and collar—size 3 (3.25 mm) 24" (60-cm) circular (cir) and set of 4 double-pointed (dpn).

Size C: Body and sleeves—size 7 (4.5 mm) 24" (60-cm) circular (cir) and set of 4 double-pointed (dpn). Bottom border, cuffs, front bands, and collar—size 4 (3.5 mm) 24" (60-cm) circular (cir) and set of 4 double-pointed (dpn).

Size D: Body and sleeves—size 8 (5 mm) 24" (60-cm) circular (cir) and set of 4 double-pointed (dpn). Bottom border, cuffs, front bands, and collar—size 5 (3.75 mm) 24" (60-cm) circular (cir) and set of 4 double-pointed (dpn).

Adjust needle size if necessary to obtain the correct gauge.

Techniques

K1f&b increase (page 137), chart reading (page 139), pick up by knitting (page 137), three-needle bind-off (page 138), backward-loop increase (page 137), short rows (page 138).

Stitch Guide

Seed Stitch *(worked over an even number of sts, both flat and circularly)*

Row/Rnd 1: (RS) *K1, p1; rep from *.

Row/Rnd 2: *P1, k1 rep from *.

Rep Rows/Rnds 1 and 2 for patt.

Seed Stitch *(Worked over an Odd Number of Stitches*

All Rows: *K1, p1; rep from * to last st, k1.

Rep this row for patt.

Notes

» The size of the jacket is determined by the needle size—the larger sizes are made using larger needles. For this reason, doing a gauge swatch is very important!

» The lower body is worked in one piece to the armholes, then the back and fronts are divided and worked separately to the shoulders.

» When working in seed stitch, always knit a stitch above a purl stitch and purl a stitch above a knit stitch.

NOTIONS

Markers (m); cable needle (cn); smooth cotton scrap yarn for holders; seven ½" (1.3 cm) buttons.

GAUGE

Size A: 22 stitches and 28 rows = 4" (10 cm) in stockinette using larger needles; 28 stitches and 34 rows = 4" (10 cm) in Cable and Rib pattern from chart using larger needles.

Size B: 20 stitches and 26 rows = 4" (10 cm) in stockinette using larger needles; 26 stitches and 34 rows = 4" (10 cm) in Cable and Rib pattern from chart using larger needles.

Size C: 18 stitches and 24 rows = 4" (10 cm) in stockinette using larger needles; 24 stitches and 32 rows = 4" (10 cm) in Cable and Rib pattern from chart using larger needles.

Size D: 17 stitches and 22 rows = 4" (10 cm) in stockinette using larger needles; 22 stitches and 30 rows = 4" (10 cm) in Cable and Rib pattern from chart using larger needles.

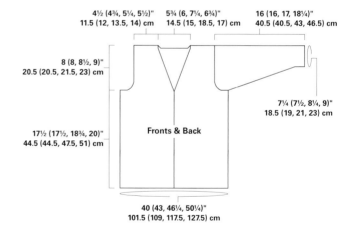

4½ (4¾, 5¼, 5½)"
11.5 (12, 13.5, 14) cm

5¾ (6, 7¼, 6¾)"
14.5 (15, 18.5, 17) cm

16 (16, 17, 18¼)"
40.5 (40.5, 43, 46.5) cm

8 (8, 8½, 9)"
20.5 (20.5, 21.5, 23) cm

7¼ (7½, 8¼, 9)"
18.5 (19, 21, 23) cm

17½ (17½, 18¾, 20)"
44.5 (44.5, 47.5, 51) cm

Fronts & Back

40 (43, 46¼, 50¼)"
101.5 (109, 117.5, 127.5) cm

LOWER BODY

Bottom Border

With smaller 24" (60-cm) cir, CO 238 sts for all sizes. Work in seed st (see Stitch Guide) for 9 rows, beg and ending with a RS row. **Next row:** (WS) Work 6 sts in established seed st, k1f&b, work 3 seed sts, k1f&b, [work 12 seed sts, k1f&b, work 3 seed sts, k1f&b] 13 times, work 6 seed sts—266 sts; piece measures about 1¼ (1¼, 1¼, 1½)" (3.2 [3.2, 3.2, 3.8] cm) from CO.

Body

Change to larger 24" (60-cm) cir. Beg and ending where indicated for lower body, rep Rows 1–4 of Cable and Rib chart 34 times, then work Rows 1 and 2 once more—138 chart rows completed. **Next row:** (RS, Row 3 of chart) Work 66 sts in established patt for right front, place marker (pm) for right side, work 134 sts for back, pm for left side, work 66 sts in patt for left front.

Reserve Underarms and Fronts

Next row: (WS, Row 4 of chart) Work in patt to 9 sts past the first m, place the last 17 sts (including marker) on holder for left armhole, work in patt to 8 sts past the second m, place the last 17 sts worked (including marker) on holder for right armhole, work to end of row—58 sts each for right and left fronts; 116 sts for back; center st on each underarm holder is the st in between the two cables; 140 chart rows completed; piece measures about 17½ (17½, 18¾, 20)" (44.5 [44.5, 47.5, 51] cm) from CO. Break yarn. Place both fronts on holders.

BACK

Rejoin yarn to 116 back sts on needle with RS facing. **Dec row:** (RS) K1, ssk, work in established patt to last 3 sts, k2tog, k1—2 sts dec'd. Continuing in established patt, rep the dec row on the next 2 RS rows—110 sts. Continue in patt until 64 rows (16 full patt reps) of chart have been completed above underarm.

Right Back Neck Shaping

Row 1: (RS, Row 1 of chart) Work 34 sts in patt, k2tog, k1, place center 36 sts on holder for back neck, place rem 37 sts on holder for left shoulder—36 right shoulder sts rem on needle.

Row 2: (WS) Working on right shoulder sts only, work to end in patt.

Row 3: Work in patt to last 3 sts, k2tog, k1—35 sts.

Row 4: Work 5 sts in patt, p2tog, p3, p2tog, work 12 sts in patt, p2tog, p3, p2tog, work 4 sts in patt—31 sts rem for right shoulder; 68 rows total completed above underarm, piece measures about 8 (8, 8½, 9) (20.5 [20.5, 21.5, 23] cm) above underarm. Break yarn. Place sts on holder.

Cable and Rib

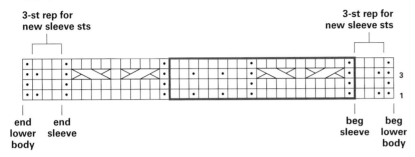

3-st rep for new sleeve sts

3-st rep for new sleeve sts

end lower body

end sleeve

beg sleeve

beg lower body

☐ k on RS rows and all rnds; p on WS rows

· p on RS rows and all rnds; k on WS rows

☐ pattern repeat

sl 2 sts onto cn and hold in back, k2, k2 from cn

sl 2 sts onto cn and hold in front, k2, k2 from cn

Left Back Neck Shaping

Place 37 sts for left back shoulder on larger cir, leaving center 36 sts on holder. Rejoin yarn to left shoulder sts with RS facing.

Row 1: (RS, Row 3 of chart) K1, ssk, work to end in patt—36 sts.

Row 2: Work to end in patt.

Row 3: K1, ssk , work to end in patt—35 sts.

Row 4: Work 4 sts in patt, p2tog, p3, p2tog, work 12 sts in patt, p2tog, p3, p2tog, work 5 sts in patt—31 sts rem for left shoulder; 68 rows total completed above underarm, piece same as right back neck above underarm. Break yarn. Place sts on holder.

LEFT FRONT

Place 58 held sts of left front on larger cir and rejoin yarn with RS facing at armhole edge. Pm in knitting at end of row (neck edge) to indicate start of neck shaping.

Row 1: (RS, Row 1 of chart) K1, ssk, work in patt to last 3 sts, k2tog, k1—2 sts dec'd; 1 st each at armhole and neck edge.

Rows 2 and 4: Work even in patt.

Row 3: K1, ssk, work in patt to end—1 st dec'd at armhole edge.

Row 5: Rep Row 1—53 sts; all armhole shaping has been completed.

Continuing in patt, dec 1 st at neck edge 18 more times by working last 3 sts of RS rows as k2tog, k1 as foll: [Work 1 WS row even, work RS neck dec row, work 3 rows even, work RS neck dec row] 9 times—35 sts. Work 8 rows even in patt, ending with RS Row 3 of chart; 67 chart rows completed above underarm. **Next row:** (WS) Work 5 sts in patt, p2tog, p3, p2tog, work 12 sts in patt, p2tog, p3, p2tog, 4 sts in patt—31 sts rem; 68 rows total completed above underarm, piece measures same as back above underarm. Break yarn. Place sts on holder.

RIGHT FRONT

Place 58 held sts of right front on larger cir and rejoin yarn with RS facing at neck edge. Pm in knitting at beg of row (neck edge) to indicate start of neck shaping.

Row 1: (RS, Row 1 of chart) K1, ssk, work in patt to last 3 sts, k2tog, k1—2 sts dec'd; 1 st each at armhole and neck edge.

Rows 2 and 4: Work even in patt.

Row 3: Work in patt to last 3 sts, k2tog, k1—1 st dec'd at armhole edge.

Row 5: Rep Row 1—53 sts; all armhole shaping has been completed.

Continuing in patt, dec 1 st at neck edge 18 more times by working first 3 sts of RS rows as k1, ssk as foll: [Work 1 WS row even, work RS neck dec row, work 3 rows even, work RS neck dec row] 9 times—35 sts. Work 8 rows even in patt, ending with RS Row 3 of chart; 67 chart rows completed above underarm. Next row: (WS) Work 4 sts in patt, p2tog, p3, p2tog, work 12 sts in patt, p2tog, p3, p2tog, work in patt to end—31 sts rem; 68 rows total completed above underarm, piece same as back above underarm. Break yarn. Place sts on holder.

JOIN SHOULDERS

With RS of pieces touching and WS facing outward, join 31 front and back shoulder sts using the three-needle bind-off method.

SLEEVES

Notes: Sleeves are worked in the round from cuffs upward, then attached to the body by binding off the live sleeve sts tog with stitches picked up around the armhole opening using the three-needle bind-off method. The main Cable and Rib pattern is centered on the sleeve, and new stitches at each side are worked in the repeating 3-stitch rib patterns marked for the sleeve on each side of the chart. Because the sleeve is knit in the round, read all chart rows from right to left as RS rounds.

Cuff

With smaller dpn, CO 44 sts. Join for working in the rnd, and pm for beg of rnd. Work in seed st for 10 rnds, inc 6 sts evenly spaced in last rnd—50 sts; piece measures about 1¼ (1¼, 1¼, 1½)" (3.2 [3.2, 3.2, 3.8] cm) from CO.

Sleeve Shaping

Change to larger dpn. Beg and ending where indicated for sleeve, establish patt from Rnd 1 of Cable and Rib chart as foll: K1, work 19-st patt rep box 2 times, work 11 sts after patt rep box once. **Note:** Work the first st of every rnd as k1 (not shown on chart); shaping increases will be

worked on each side of this knit st. Work 3 more rnds in established patt. **Inc rnd:** Using the backward-loop method for all incs, k1, inc 1, work in patt to end, inc 1—2 sts inc'd. Continuing in established patt, rep the inc rnd every 5th rnd 20 times, then every 4th round 5 times, working new sts into 3-st rib patts marked on chart at each side of sleeve sts—102 sts; 125 chart rnds completed above cuff; piece measures about 16 (16, 17, 18¼)" (40.5 [40.5, 43, 46.5] cm) from CO. Place sts on holder or leave on needles if attaching to body immediately.

Set up Armholes and Attach Sleeves

Note: Leave underarm holder strings in place until after the underarm sts have been attached, then remove holders. With larger cir and RS facing, beg at st in middle of underarm work 9 held underarm sts as k2tog, k7, pick up by knitting 43 sts along armhole edge to shoulder, then 43 sts down to underarm, k8 rem held underarm sts—102 sts. With RS of pieces touching and WS facing outward, beg at underarm m, join 102 live sts at top of sleeve to 102 sts picked up around armhole using the three-needle bind-off method.

FINISHING
Right Front Band and Lapel

Pm on right front neck edge about 17 rows down from shoulder join. With smaller 24" (60-cm) needle and RS facing, beg at CO edge of right front pick up by knitting 100 sts along front edge from CO to m for beg of neck shaping, then 33 sts along shaped right front neck to second m—133 sts.

Right Lapel Shaping

The lapel is shaped using short-rows; if you are accustomed to working wrapped stitches together with their wraps, it is not necessary to do so in seed stitch; simply work each wrapped stitch in pattern as you come to it. **Tip:** The row number equals the number of stitches to work in seed stitch before each wrap and turn.

Short-row 1: (WS) Sl 1 st as if to purl with yarn in front (pwise wyf), k1, wrap next st and turn (WT)—wrapped st is 3rd st of row.

Even-numbered Short-rows 2–30: (RS) Work in seed st to last st, k1.

Short-row 3: Sl 1 pwise wyf, work 3 sts in established seed st, WT—wrapped st is 5th st of row.

Short-row 5: Sl 1 pwise wyf, work 5 sts in established seed st, WT—wrapped st is 7th st of row.

Odd-numbered Short-rows 7–31: Continue in this manner, working 2 more seed sts in each row before WT—last wrapped st in Short-row 31 is at m at start of neck shaping.

Short-row 32: (RS) Work in seed st to last st, k1.

Right Front Border and Buttonholes

Work back and forth across all 133 sts as foll:

Row 1 and 3: (WS) Sl 1 pwise wyf, work in seed st as established to end.

Row 2: Work in seed st as established to last st, k1.

Row 4: (RS, buttonhole row) Work 4 sts in established seed st, [k2tog, yo, work 13 seed sts] 6 times, k2tog, yo, work in patt to last st, k1—7 buttonholes completed.

Rows 5–9: Rep Rows 1 and 2 two times, then work Row 1 once more. BO loosely in patt.

Left Front Band and Lapel

Pm on left front neck edge about 17 rows down from shoulder join. With smaller 24" (60-cm) needle and RS facing, beg at upper m on left front, pick up by knitting 33 sts along shaped left front neck between m, then 100 sts along left front to CO edge—133 sts.

Left Lapel Shaping

Set-up Row: (WS) Work in seed st to last st, sl 1 pwise wyf.

Short-row 1: (RS) K1, work 1 st in established seed st, wrap next st and turn (WT)—wrapped st is 3rd st of row.

Even-numbered Short-rows 2–30: (WS) Work in seed st to last st, sl 1 pwise wyf.

Short-row 3: K1, work 3 sts in established seed st, WT—wrapped st is 5th st of row.

Short-row 5: Sl 1 pwise wyf, work 5 sts in established seed st, WT—wrapped st is 7th st of row.

Odd-numbered Short-rows 7-31: Continue in this manner, working 2 more seed sts in each row before WT—last wrapped st in Short-row 31 is at m at start of neck shaping.

Short-row 32: (WS) Work in seed st to last st, sl 1 pwise wyf.

Left Front Border

Work back and forth across all 133 sts as foll:

Row 1: (RS) K1, work in seed st as established to end.

Row 2: Work in seed st as established to last st, sl 1 pwise wyf.

Rows 3–9: Rep Rows 1 and 2 three times, then work Row 1 once more. BO loosely in patt.

Collar

With smaller 24" (60-cm) needle and WS of garment facing (RS of lapel when folded back), beg in the 11th slipped selvedge st from bound-off edge of left lapel, pick up by knitting 12 sts along slipped lapel selvedge, 12 sts along left front neck edge to shoulder join, 5 sts along left back neck shaping, k36 held back neck sts, pick up 5 sts along right back neck shaping, 12 sts along right from neck edge to right lapel, and 12 sts along slip st selvedge of right lapel—94 sts. **Next row:** Sl 1 pwise wyf, work in seed st to last st, k1. Rep the last row 21 more times, BO in patt.

Sew buttons into place on left front to correspond to buttonholes.

During the Edo period in Japan (1603 to 1868), art and culture flourished. Haiku poetry was born, focusing on themes of simplicity and beauty found in everyday life. The style of the knitted lace Edo is based on the traditionally simple Japanese hanten jacket.

Edo

"Traveling this high mountain trail, delighted by violets."

—Bashō, Edo-period poet

FINISHED SIZE

Size A: 53½" (136 cm) chest circumference

Size B: 58" (147.5 cm) chest circumference

Jacket shown measures 58" (147.5 cm). Edo has a relaxed, flowing, oversize fit (see fit guidelines on page 136).

YARN (4)

Shown here: Cheryl Oberle's Reflections Hand-dyed (55% mohair, 45% merino; about 325 yd [297 m]/8 oz [227 g]): Pewter, 4 hanks for both sizes.

NEEDLES

Size A: Body and sleeves—size 9 (5.5 mm) 24" (60-cm) circular needle (cir). Bottom border, front and neck border, and sleeve cuffs—size 7 (4.5 mm) 24" (60-cm) cir.

Size B: Body and sleeves—size 10 (6 mm) 24" (60-cm) circular needle (cir). Bottom border, front and neck border, and sleeve cuffs—size 8 (5 mm).

Adjust needle size if necessary to obtain the correct gauge (see Notes next page).

NOTIONS

Markers (m; several of each in 2 different colors); smooth cotton scrap yarn for holders.

GAUGE

Size A: 15 stitches and 23 rows = 4" (10 cm) in stockinette using larger needle; 12 stitches and 20 rows = 4" (10 cm) in lace patterns using larger needle, after blocking (see Notes next page).

Size B: 14 stitches and 22 rows = 4" (10 cm) in stockinette using larger needle; 11 stitches and 17 rows = 4" (10 cm) in lace patterns using larger needle, after blocking (see Notes next page).

Techniques

Three-needle bind-off (page 138), pick up by knitting (page 137).

Stitch Guide

Lace Pattern for Body *(worked over 140 sts)*

Row 1: (RS) K2, [yo, ssk] 5 times, *k5, [yo, ssk] 5 times; rep from * 2 more times; k5, [yo, ssk] 8 times for center back sts, **k5, [yo, ssk] 5 times; rep from ** 3 more times, k2.

Row 2: (WS) **Note:** To help keep track of the lace panels, place markers (pm) on the needle before each k3 in this row, using different-color markers from the ones used to mark the sides of the piece. P13, [pm, k3, p12] 3 times, pm, k3, p18, [pm, k3, p12] 4 times, p1.

Row 3: K2, [k2tog, yo] 5 times,*k5, [k2tog, yo] 5 times; rep from *2 more times; k5, [k2tog, yo] 8 times for center back sts; **k5, [k2tog, yo] 5 times; rep from ** 3 more times, k2.

Row 4: P13, [k3, p12] 3 times, k3, p18, [k3, p12] 4 times, p1.

Rep Rows 1–4 for patt.

Lace Pattern for Sleeves
(multiple of 15 sts, plus 14)

Row 1: (RS) K2, [yo, ssk] 5 times, *k5, [yo, ssk] 5 times; rep from * to last 2 sts, k2.

Row 2: (WS) **Note:** As for body, pm on the needle before each k3 in this row. P13, *pm, k3, p12; rep from * to last st, p1.

Row 3: K2, [k2tog, yo] 5 times,*k5, [k2tog, yo] 5 times; rep from * to last 2 sts, k2.

Row 4: P13, *k3, p12; rep from * to last st, p1.

Rep Rows 1–4 for patt.

Notes

» The size of the jacket is determined by the needle size—the larger size is made using larger needles. For this reason, doing a gauge swatch is very important!

» Remember that knitted lace blocks out to be much more open (and thus larger) than it appears as you knit. For this reason, the measurements will not conform to the schematic measurements as the jacket comes off the needles—block the jacket to achieve the proper size. This makes doing that gauge swatch even more important!

» The lower body is worked in one piece to the armholes, then the back and fronts are divided and worked separately to the shoulders.

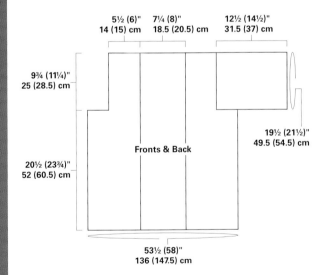

5½ (6)"
14 (15) cm

7¼ (8)"
18.5 (20.5) cm

12½ (14½)"
31.5 (37) cm

9¾ (11¼)"
25 (28.5) cm

19½ (21½)"
49.5 (54.5) cm

20½ (23¾)"
52 (60.5) cm

Fronts & Back

53½ (58)"
136 (147.5) cm

LOWER BODY

Bottom Border

With smaller cir, CO 140 sts very loosely for both sizes. Work in garter st (knit all sts every row) for 9 rows, beg and ending with a RS row. **Next row:** (WS) Knit, placing markers (pm) as foll: K29 for left front, pm for left side, k82 for back, pm for right side, k29 for right front.

Body

Change to larger cir and Lace Pattern for Body (see Stitch Guide). Repeat Rows 1–4 of patt 23 times, then work Rows 1–3 once more, ending with a RS row.

Reserve Underarms and Fronts

Next row: (WS, Row 4 of patt) Work in patt as established to 13 sts past the left side m, place the last 25 sts worked on holder for left armhole (leaving m in place), work in patt to 12 sts past the right side m, place the last 25 sts worked (including m) on holder for right armhole, work in patt to end of row—17 sts each for right and left fronts; 56 sts for back; 96 patt rows completed; center 3 sts on each holder are 3 garter sts. Break yarn. Place both fronts on holders.

BACK

Rejoin yarn to 56 back sts on needle with RS facing. Continuing in established patt, rep Rows 1–4 twelve more times—48 patt rows completed above the underarm. Place sts on holder.

LEFT FRONT

Place 17 left front sts on larger cir and rejoin yarn with RS facing at armhole edge. Continuing in established patt, rep Rows 1–4 twelve more times—48 patt rows completed above the underarm. Place sts on holder.

RIGHT FRONT

Place 17 right front sts on larger cir and rejoin yarn with RS facing at neck edge. Continuing in established patt, rep Rows 1–4 twelve more times—48 patt rows completed above the underarm. Place sts on holder.

SLEEVES

Notes: Sleeves are worked back and forth in rows, then attached to the body by binding off the live sleeve sts tog with sts picked up around the armhole opening using the three-needle bind-off method. The held underarm sts are

bound off, then sewn to the sleeve selvedges during finishing to form a square, set-in armhole and a type of underarm gusset. With smaller cir, CO 59 sts. Work in garter st for 10 rows, ending with a WS row. Change to larger cir. Rep Rows 1–4 of Lace Pattern for Sleeves (see Stitch Guide) 14 times, ending with WS Row 4—56 patt rows completed. Place sts on holder.

Join Shoulders

With RS of pieces touching and WS facing outward, join 17 front and back shoulder sts using the three-needle bind-off method—22 sts rem on holder for center back neck.

Set up Armholes and Attach Sleeves

Place 25 held underarm sts on larger cir and rejoin yarn with RS facing. BO sts loosely as if to knit. With larger cir and RS facing, beg at bottom of armhole pick up by knitting 29 sts along armhole selvedge to shoulder join, 1 st in join, then 29 sts along other armhole selvedge to end at bottom of armhole—59 sts picked up. With WS of pieces touching and RS facing outward, beg at underarm m, join 59 lives sts at top of sleeve to 59 sts picked up around armhole using the three-needle bind-off method. The bind-off ridge will form a decorative welt on the outside of the garment.

Form Underarm Gussets and Finish Sleeves

Sew the top 4¼ (4½)" (11 [11.5] cm) of each sleeve selvedge to bound-off underarm sts, working from the corners of the armhole "notches" to center of underarm sts, then finish sewing each sleeve seam down to the cuff.

FINISHING
Front and Neck Borders

With smaller cir needle and RS facing, beg at lower edge of right front pick up by knitting 105 sts along right front to shoulder join, k22 from back neck holder, then pick up by knitting 105 sts along left front from the shoulder to lower edge of left front—232 sts.

Rows 1–5: Knit.
Row 6: (RS) K2, *yo, ssk; repeat from * to last 2 sts, k2.
Row 7: Purl.
Row 8: K2, *k2tog, yo; repeat from * to last 2 sts, k2.
Row 9: Purl.
Rows 10–13: Knit.
Rows 14–17: Rep Row 6–9 once more.
Rows 18–22: Knit.

BO loosely. **Tip**: BO using a larger needle to keep bind-off loose and flexible.

Little Edo has more in common with Edo than just a name. Though both are knitted with the same number of stitches, utilizing the same simple pattern and yarn, the variation in gauge and body length creates the difference in style. With fewer rows and smaller needles, Little Edo is a more fitted, cropped version of the Edo Jacket. What a little change can do!

Little Edo

"Where there is laughter happiness likes to be."

—Japanese proverb

FINISHED SIZE
Size A: 46¾" (118.5 cm) chest circumference
Size B: 50½" (128.5 cm) chest circumference
Jacket shown measures 46¾" (118.5 cm). Little Edo is loose fitting (see fit guidelines on page 136).

YARN 4
Shown here: Cheryl Oberle's Reflections Hand-dyed (55% mohair, 45% merino; about 325 yd [297 m]/8 oz [227 g]): Iris, 3 hanks for both sizes.

NEEDLES
Size A: Body and sleeves—size 7 (4.5 mm) 24" (60-cm) circular needle (cir). Bottom border, front and neck border, and sleeve cuffs—size 5 (3.75 mm) 24" (60-cm) cir.

Size B: Body and sleeves—size 8 (5 mm) 24" (60-cm) circular needle (cir). Bottom border, front and neck border, and sleeve cuffs—size 6 (4 mm) 24" (60-cm) cir.

Adjust needle size if necessary to obtain the correct gauge (see Notes next page).

NOTIONS
Markers (m; several of each in 2 different colors); smooth cotton scrap yarn for holders.

GAUGE
Size A: 18 stitches and 26 rows = 4" (10 cm) in stockinette using larger needle; 14 stitches and 23 rows = 4" (10 cm) in lace patterns using larger needle (see Notes next page).

Size B: 17 stitches and 25 rows = 4" (10 cm) in stockinette using larger needle; 13 stitches and 21 rows = 4" (10 cm) in lace patterns using larger needle (see Notes next page).

Techniques

Three-needle bind-off (page 138), pick up by knitting (page 137).

Stitch Guide

See Edo (page 106) for lace patterns.

Notes

» The size of the jacket is determined by the needle size—the larger size is made using larger needles. For this reason, doing a gauge swatch is very important!

» Remember that knitted lace blocks out to be much more open (and thus larger) than it appears as you knit. For this reason, the measurements as the jacket comes off the needles—block the jacket to achieve the proper size. This makes doing that gauge swatch even more important!

» The lower body is worked in one piece to the armholes, then the back and fronts are divided and worked separately to the shoulders.

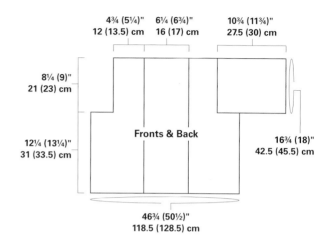

4¾ (5¼)" 6¼ (6¾)" 10¾ (11¾)"
12 (13.5) cm 16 (17) cm 27.5 (30) cm

8¼ (9)"
21 (23) cm

Fronts & Back

16¾ (18)"
42.5 (45.5) cm

12¼ (13¼)"
31 (33.5) cm

46¾ (50½)"
118.5 (128.5) cm

LOWER BODY

Using the gauges given on page 111, work as for Edo (page 107) with this exception: After completing the garter stitch bottom border, change to larger cir and rep Rows 1–4 of Lace Pattern for Body only 15 times, then work Rows 1–3 once more, ending with a RS row. Reserve underarms and fronts as for Edo.

BACK, LEFT FRONT, RIGHT FRONT, AND SLEEVES

Work as for Edo.

FINISHING

Front and Neck Borders

With smaller cir needle and RS facing, beg at lower edge of right front pick up by knitting 67 sts along right front to shoulder join, k22 from back neck holder, then pick up by knitting 67 sts along left front from the shoulder to lower edge of left front—156 sts. Work Rows 1–22 of front and neck borders as for Edo. BO loosely.

The cropped structure of Ivory Leaves lends the air of a knitted lace shawl to a simple jacket. The appeal of knitted lace is due largely to the texture of the fabric. In leaf lace motifs, the hard edges of interlocking diamonds are shaped by the decreases and yarnovers into pleasing curves. Knitting lace in heavier yarns accentuates the rich textures.

Ivory Leaves

"A leaf fluttered in through the window this morning, as if supported by the rays of the sun, a bird settled on the fire escape, joy in the task of coffee, joy accompanied me as I walked."

—Anaïs Nin

FINISHED SIZE

Size A: 47½" (120.5) chest circumference

Size B: 50½" (128.5 cm) chest circumference

Size C: 54" (137 cm) chest circumference

Jacket shown measures 47½" (120.5 cm). Ivory Leaves is oversize (see fit guidelines on page 136).

YARN 4

Shown in: Henry's Attic Texas Big Horn (55% mohair, 45% merino; 325 yd [297 m]/8 oz [227 g]): Natural, 3 hanks.

NEEDLES

Size A: Body and sleeves—size 7 (4.5 mm) 24" and 16" (60- and 40-cm) circular needles (cir). Bottom border, cuffs, and front border—size 5 (3.75 mm) 24" and 16" (60- and 40-cm) cir.

Size B: Body and sleeves—size 8 (5 mm) 24" and 16" (60- and 40-cm) circular needles (cir). Bottom border, cuffs, and front border—size 6 (4 mm) 24" and 16" (60- and 40-cm) cir.

Size C: Body and sleeves—size 9 (5.5 mm) 24" and 16" (60- and 40-cm) circular needles (cir). Bottom border, cuffs, and front border—size 7 (4.5 mm) 24" and 16" (60- and 40-cm) cir.

Adjust needle size if necessary obtain the correct gauge.

NOTIONS

Markers (m); smooth cotton scrap yarn for holders.

Techniques

Three-needle bind-off (page 138), chart reading (page 139), pick up by knitting (page 137).

Notes

» The size of the jacket is determined by the needle size—the larger sizes are made using larger needles. For this reason, doing a gauge swatch is very important!

» Remember that knitted lace blocks out to be much more open (and thus larger) than it appears as you knit. For this reason, the measurements will not conform to the schematic measurements as the jacket comes off the needles—block the jacket to achieve the proper size. This makes doing that gauge swatch even more important!

» The lower body is worked in one piece to the armholes, then the back and fronts are divided and worked separately to the shoulders.

GAUGE

Size A: 18 stitches and 26 rows = 4" (10 cm) in stockinette using larger needle; 17 stitches and 21 rows = 4" (10 cm) in Ivory Leaves pattern from chart using larger needle.

Size B: 17 stitches and 25 rows = 4" (10 cm) in stockinette using larger needle; 16 stitches and 20 rows = 4" (10 cm) in Ivory Leaves pattern from chart using larger needle.

Size C: 16 stitches and 24 rows = 4" (10 cm) in stockinette using larger needle; 15 stitches and 19 rows = 4" (10 cm) in Ivory Leaves pattern from chart using larger needle.

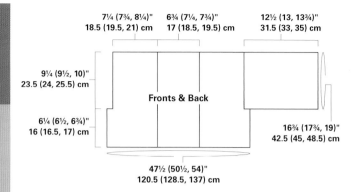

7¼ (7¾, 8¼)"
18.5 (19.5, 21) cm

6¾ (7¼, 7¾)"
17 (18.5, 19.5) cm

12½ (13, 13¾)"
31.5 (33, 35) cm

9¼ (9½, 10)"
23.5 (24, 25.5) cm

Fronts & Back

6¼ (6½, 6¾)"
16 (16.5, 17) cm

16¾ (17¾, 19)"
42.5 (45, 48.5) cm

47½ (50½, 54)"
120.5 (128.5, 137) cm

LOWER BODY

Bottom Border

With smaller 24" (60-cm) cir, very loosely CO 171 sts for all sizes. Work 4 rows of garter st (knit all sts every row) ending with a WS row.

Body

Change to larger 24" (60-cm) cir. Work Rows 1–24 of Ivory Leaves patt from chart once, then work Rows 1–4 once more—28 chart rows completed above bottom border. **Next row:** (RS, Row 5 of chart) Work 35 sts in established patt for right front, place marker (pm) for right side, work 101 sts in patt for back, pm for left side, work 35 sts in patt for left front.

Reserve Underarms and Fronts

Next row: (WS, Row 6 of chart) Work in patt as established to 5 sts past the left side m, place the last 9 sts worked on holder for left armhole (leaving m in place), work in patt to 4 sts past the right side m, place the last 9 sts worked (including m) on a holder for right armhole, work in patt to end of row—31 sts each for right and left fronts; 91 sts for back; 30 chart rows completed. Break yarn. Place both fronts on holders.

Ivory Leaves

(chart: rows 1–23 odd numbered shown at right of grid; "Note: Only RS pattern rows are charted.")

Legend:

- ☐ k on RS rows and all rnds; p on WS rows
- • p on RS rows and all rnds; k on WS rows
- ○ yo
- ╱ k2tog
- ╲ ssk
- ☐ pattern repeat

Note: Only RS pattern rows are charted.

When working flat, purl all
even-numbered WS rows, including 24.

When working circularly, knit all
even-numbered rounds.

BACK

Rejoin yarn to 91 back sts on needle with RS facing.
Continuing in established patt, work Rows 7–24 of chart
once, work Rows 1–24 once, then work Rows 1–6 once
more—78 chart rows (3 full patt reps plus 6 rows) completed. Place sts on holder.

LEFT FRONT

Place 31 held left front sts on larger 24" (60-cm) cir and
rejoin yarn with RS facing at armhole edge. Continue in established patt until the left front contains the same number
of rows as the back. Place sts on holder.

RIGHT FRONT

Place 31 held right front sts on larger 24" (60-cm) cir and
rejoin yarn with RS facing at neck edge. Continue in established patt until right front contains the same number of
rows as the back and left front. Place sts on holder.

JOIN SHOULDERS

With RS of pieces touching and WS facing outward, join 31 front and back shoulder sts using the three-needle bind-off method—29 sts rem on holder for center back neck.

SLEEVES

Notes: Sleeves are worked in the round from cuffs upward, then attached to the body by binding off the live sleeve stitches together with stitches picked up around the arm-hole opening using the three-needle bind-off method. Read all chart rows from right to left as RS rounds. With smaller 16" (40-cm) cir, CO 71 sts. Join for working in the rnd, and pm for beg of rnd. Work garter st in the rnd as foll:

Rnd 1: Purl.

Rnd 2: Knit.

Rep these 2 rnds 4 more times, then work Rnd 1 once more—11 rnds garter st completed. Change to larger 16" (40-cm) cir. Rep Rnds 1–24 of Ivory Leaves chart 2 times, then work Rnds 1–10 once more—58 chart rnds completed. Place sts on holder.

Set up Armholes and Attach Sleeves

Note: Leave underarm holder strings in place until after the underarm sts have been attached, then remove holders. With larger 16" (40-cm) cir and RS facing, beg at m in center of held underarm sts, pick up by knitting 71 sts around armhole, including underarm sts. With RS of pieces touching and WS facing outward, join 71 live sts at top of sleeve to 71 sts picked up around armhole using the three-needle bind-off method.

FINISHING

Front Border

With smaller 24" (60-cm) cir and RS facing, beg at CO edge of right front pick up by knitting 55 sts along right front to shoulder join, k29 held back neck sts, pick up 55 sts along left front from shoulder join to CO edge of left front—139 sts.

Row 1: (WS) Knit.

Rows 2 and 3: Knit.

Row 4: (RS) K1, *yo, k2tog; rep from *.

Rows 5–9: Knit.

Row 10: K1, *yo, k2tog; rep from *.

Rows 11–13: Knit.

Row 14: K1, *yo, k2tog; rep from *.

Rows 15–25: Knit.

BO loosely.

Alternating columns of stockinette stitch and cables give Scholar's Jacket a classic style reminiscent of the grand stone facade of a venerable library or museum. The pockets, high ribbed neck, and seed stitch side panels give it character and comfort. With an interesting construction, pocket openings are created as the body is knit and then the pockets are knit on the inside.

Scholar's Jacket

"The important thing is not to stop questioning."

—Albert Einstein

FINISHED SIZE

Size A: 43¾" (111 cm) chest circumference

Size B: 46¾" (118.5 cm) chest circumference

Size C: 50" (127 cm) chest circumference

Jacket shown measures 46¾" (118.5 cm). Scholar's Jacket is loose fitting (see fit guidelines on page 136).

YARN 4

Shown here: Philosopher's Wool 2-ply Worsted (100% wool; 200 yd [183 m]/4 oz [113 g]): Dark Green Heather, 8 (8, 9) skeins.

NEEDLES

Size A: Body, sleeves, pockets, and pocket bands—size 7 (4.5 mm) 24" and 16" (60- and 40-cm) circular (cir), and set of 4 double-pointed (dpn). Bottom ribbing, cuffs, front bands, and neckband—size 5 (3.75 mm) 24" (60-cm) circular (cir) and set of 4 double-pointed (dpn).

Size B: Body, sleeves, pockets, and pocket bands—size 8 (5 mm) 24" and 16" (60- and 40-cm) circular (cir), and set of 4 double-pointed (dpn). Bottom ribbing, cuffs, front bands, and neckband—size 6 (4 mm) 24" (60-cm) circular (cir) and set of 4 double-pointed (dpn).

Size C: Body, sleeves, pockets, and pocket bands—size 9 (5.5 mm) 24" and 16" (60- and 40-cm) circular (cir), and set of 4 double-pointed (dpn). Bottom ribbing, cuffs, front bands, and neckband—size 7 (4.5 mm) 24" (60-cm) circular (cir) and set of 4 double-pointed (dpn).

Adjust needle size if necessary to obtain the correct gauge (see Notes next page).

NOTIONS

Markers (m; several of each in 2 different colors); cable needle (cn); smooth cotton scrap yarn for holders; six ⅝" (1.6 cm) buttons.

Techniques

Backward-loop increase (page 137), chart reading (page 139), three-needle bind-off (page 138), pick up by knitting (page 137).

Stitch Guide

K1, P1 Rib *(worked over an even number of sts)*

All Rows: *K1, p1; rep from *.

Rep this row for patt.

Seed Stitch *(worked over any number of sts)*

Row 1: *K1, p1; rep from *, ending k1 if the number of sts is odd.

Row 2: Beg with k1 if the number of sts is odd, then *p1, k1; rep from * to end.

Rep Rows 1 and 2 for patt.

Tip: When working in seed stitch, always knit a stitch above a purl stitch and purl a stitch above a knit stitch.

Notes

» The size of the jacket is determined by the needle size—the larger sizes are made using larger needles. For this reason, doing a gauge swatch is very important!

» The lower body is worked in one piece to the bottom edge of the pocket slits, then divided into separate sections to create the vertical pocket openings. The lower body is joined and worked in one piece again above the pockets until the armholes, then the back and fronts are divided and worked separately to the shoulders.

» Stitches are increased in the last row of bottom ribbing to accommodate the cables.

GAUGE

Size A: 17 stitches and 27 rows = 4" (10 cm) in stockinette using larger needles; 20-st cable panel from chart measures about 3½" (9 cm) wide using larger needles.

Size B: 16 stitches and 25 rows = 4" (10 cm) in stockinette using larger needles; 20-st cable panel from chart measures about 3¾" (9.5 cm) wide using larger needles.

Size C: 15 stitches and 24 rows = 4" (10 cm) in stockinette using larger needles; 20-st cable panel from chart measures about 4" (10 cm) wide using larger needles.

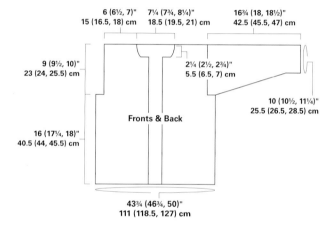

6 (6½, 7)"
15 (16.5, 18) cm

7¼ (7¾, 8¼)"
18.5 (19.5, 21) cm

16¾ (18, 18½)"
42.5 (45.5, 47) cm

9 (9½, 10)"
23 (24, 25.5) cm

2¼ (2½, 2¾)"
5.5 (6.5, 7) cm

10 (10½, 11¼)"
25.5 (26.5, 28.5) cm

Fronts & Back

16 (17¼, 18)"
40.5 (44, 45.5) cm

43¾ (46¾, 50)"
111 (118.5, 127) cm

LOWER BODY

Bottom Ribbing

With smaller 24" (60-cm) cir, CO 192 sts for all sizes. Work in K1, P1 Rib (see Stitch Guide) for 5 rows, beg and ending with a WS row. **Inc row:** (RS) Using the backward-loop method for all incs, work 14 sts in established rib, place marker (pm), [work 4 rib sts, inc 1, work 10 rib sts, inc 1, work 4 rib sts], pm, work 7 rib sts, pm, work 6 rib sts, pm in different color for right side, work 5 rib sts, pm, work 7 rib sts, pm, work 18 sts in [ ] once more inc them to 20 sts, pm, work 12 rib sts, pm, work 18 sts in [ ] once more inc them to 20 sts, pm, work 12 rib sts, pm, work 18 sts in [ ] once more inc them to 20 sts, pm, work 7 rib sts, pm, work 5 rib sts, pm in a different color for left side, work 6 rib sts, pm, work 7 rib sts, pm, work 18 sts in [ ] once more inc them to 20 sts, pm, work 14 rib sts—202 sts; 47 sts each for right and left fronts; 108 sts for back.

Body

Change to larger 24" (60-cm) cir. **Set-up row:** (WS) P14 for St st, work Set-up Row of Cable chart over 20 sts, p7 for St st, work 11 seed sts (see Stitch Guide), p7 for St st, [work Set-up Row of Cable chart over 20 sts, p12] 2 times, work Set-up Row of Cable chart over 20 sts, p7 for St st, work 11 seed sts, p7 for St st, work Set-up Row of Cable chart over 20 sts, p14 for St st. Continuing seed and St sts as established, rep Rows 1–8 of chart 3 times (do not rep Set-up Row), then work Rows 1–7 once more—31 chart rows completed; 33 rows total above rib including inc and set-up rows.

Divide for Pocket Openings

Next row: (WS, Row 8 of chart) Work 36 sts in established patt, inc 1, place rem 166 sts on holder—37 left front sts. Keeping the inc'd st in St st, continue in established patts and rep Rows 1–8 of chart 3 more times, then work Rows 1–6 once more.

Next row: (RS, Row 7 of chart) K2tog, work in patt to end—36 left front sts. Work 1 WS row even (Row 8 of chart). Break yarn, and place sts on a holder. With WS facing, place next 130 held sts on needle for back and sides of fronts, and rejoin yarn—36 sts rem on holder for right front. **Next row:** (WS, Row 8 of chart) Inc 1, work in patt to end of back and side sts, inc 1—132 sts. Keeping the inc'd sts in St st, continue in established patts and rep Rows 1–8 of chart 3 more times, then work Rows 1–6 once more. **Next row:** (RS, Row 7 of chart) K2tog, work in patt to last 2 sts, k2tog—130 sts for back and sides of fronts. Work 1 WS row even (Row 8 of chart). Break yarn, and place sts on a holder. With WS facing, place 36 held sts on needle for right front, and rejoin yarn. **Next row:** (WS, Row 8 of chart) Inc 1, work in patt to end—37 sts. Keeping the inc'd st in St st, continue in established patts and rep Rows 1–8

Cable

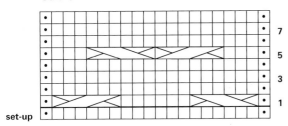

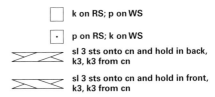

- ☐ k on RS; p on WS
- · p on RS; k on WS
- ⟋⟍ sl 3 sts onto cn and hold in back, k3, k3 from cn
- ⟍⟋ sl 3 sts onto cn and hold in front, k3, k3 from cn

of chart 3 more times, then work Rows 1–6 once more.

Next row: (RS, Row 7 of chart) Work in patt to last 2 sts, k2tog—36 right front sts. Work 1 WS row even (Row 8 of chart). Do not break yarn.

Rejoin Body

Next row: (RS, Row 1 of chart) Using working yarn attached to right front sts, work to end of right front sts, place held back and left front sts on needle, and work in patt to end of row—202 sts. Continuing in established patts, work Rows 2–8 of Cable chart once, rep Rows 1–8 of chart 3 times, then work Rows 1–3 once more.

Reserve Underarms and Fronts

Next row: (WS, Row 4 of chart) Work in patt to 5 sts past left side m, place the last 11 sts worked (the seed st panel) on holder for left armhole (including marker), work to 6 sts past right side m, place the last 11 sts worked (the seed st panel) on holder (including marker), work in patt to end—41 sts each for right and left fronts; 98 sts for back; 12½ reps of 8-row patt completed; 102 rows completed above bottom ribbing including inc and set-up rows; piece measures about 16 (17¼, 18)" (40.5 [44, 45.5] cm) from CO. Break yarn. Place both fronts on holders.

BACK

Rejoin yarn to 98 back sts on needle with RS facing. Continuing in established patts, work Rows 5–8 of chart once, then rep Rows 1–8 of chart 7 times—20 reps of 8-row patt completed from beg; 60 rows completed above underarms; piece measures about 9 (9½, 10)" (23 [24, 25.5] cm) above underarms. Place sts on holder.

LEFT FRONT

Place 41 held left front sts on larger 24" (60-cm) cir and rejoin yarn with RS facing at armhole edge. Continuing in established patts, work Rows 5–8 of chart once, then rep Rows 1–8 of chart 4 times, then work Rows 1–7 once more. Break yarn.

Next row: (WS, Row 8 of chart) Place first 7 sts on holder, rejoin yarn, work in established patts to end—34 sts; 5½ reps of 8-row patt completed above underarms.

Shape Neck

Dec row: (RS) Work in patt to last 3 sts, k2tog, k1—1 st dec'd at neck edge. Continuing in patt, work the dec row on the next 2 RS rows—31 sts. Continue in patt until 20 total reps of 8-row patt and 60 rows above underarm have been completed as for back. Place sts on holder.

RIGHT FRONT

Place 41 held right front sts on larger 24" (60-cm) cir and rejoin yarn with RS facing at neck edge. Continuing in established patts, work Rows 5–8 of chart once, then rep Rows 1–8 of chart 4 times, then work Rows 1–7 once more. **Next row:** (WS, Row 8 of chart) Work in patt to last 7 sts, then place last 7 sts on holder—34 sts; 5½ reps of 8-row patt completed above underarms.

Shape Neck

Dec row: (RS) K1, ssk, work in patt to end—1 st dec'd at neck edge. Continuing in patt, work the dec row on the next 2 RS rows—31 sts. Continue in patt until 20 total reps of 8-row patt and 60 rows above underarm have been completed as for back and left front. Place sts on holder.

JOIN SHOULDERS

With RS of pieces touching and WS facing outward, join 31 front and back shoulder sts using the three-needle bind-off method—36 sts rem on holder for center back neck.

SLEEVES

Notes: Stitches for the sleeves are picked up around the armhole and the sleeves are worked circularly down to the cuff. The first 5 and last 6 stitches of each right sleeve round, or the first 6 and last 5 stitches of each left sleeve round, are worked in seed stitch, and all shaping decreases are worked on either side of this seed-stitch panel. With larger 16" (40-cm) cir and beg at underarm m, k5 from holder for right sleeve or k6 from holder for left sleeve, pm, pick up by knitting 39 sts along armhole edge to shoulder join, 1 st in shoulder, 39 sts along armhole edge to underarm, pm, k6 rem underarm sts for right sleeve or k5 rem underarm sts for left sleeve—90 sts. Join for working in the rnd, and pm for beg of rnd. **Next rnd:** Work in seed st to m, work 79 St sts to next m, work seed st to end. Working seed and St sts as established, work 2 rnds even.

Dec rnd: Work seed st to first m, slip marker (sl m), ssk, work in St st to 2 sts before next m, k2tog, sl m, work seed st to end—2 sts dec'd. Continuing in established patts, rep the dec rnd every 4th rnd 20 more times, changing to larger dpn when there are too few sts to fit comfortably around the cir—48 sts. Work even in established patts until piece measures 14 (15¼, 15¾)" (34.5 [38.5, 40] cm) from pick-up rnd, dec 6 sts evenly spaced in last rnd—42 sts.

Cuff

Change to smaller dpn and work K1, P1 Rib for 2¾" (7 cm)—piece measures 16¾ (18, 18½)" (42.5 [45.5, 47] cm) from pick-up rnd. BO in patt.

FINISHING

Buttonband

With smaller 24" (60-cm) cir and RS facing, beg at neck edge of left front pick up by knitting 104 sts to CO edge of left front. Work in K1, P1 Rib for 18 rows. BO in patt.

Buttonhole Band

With smaller 24" (60-cm) cir and RS facing, beg at lower edge of right front pick up by knitting 104 sts to right neck edge. Work in K1, P1 Rib for 7 rows, beg and ending with a WS row. **Buttonhole row**: (RS) Work 4 rib sts, [ssk, yo, work 18 rib sts] 5 times—5 buttonholes completed. Work in rib for 10 more rows. BO in patt.

Neckband

With smaller 24" (60-cm) cir and RS facing, beg at bound-off edge of buttonhole band pick up by knitting 12 sts across band selvedge, k7 from front neck holder, pick up 11 sts along shaped right front neck, k36 from back neck holder, pick up 11 sts along shaped left front neck, k7 from front neck holder, pick up 12 sts across buttonband selvedge—96 sts. Work 1 WS row in K1, P1 Rib. **Buttonhole row**: (RS) Work 6 rib sts, ssk, yo, work in established rib to end—6th buttonhole completed. Work in rib for 16 more rows. BO in patt.

Pocket Linings and Bands

Left Pocket Lining

With larger 16" (40-cm) cir and RS facing, beg at top of left pocket opening pick up by knitting 30 sts along the back edge of pocket slit.

Row 1: (WS) P1, inc 1, purl to end—1 st inc'd at lower edge of pocket.

Row 2: Knit to last 2 sts, inc 1, k2—1 st inc'd at lower edge of pocket.

Rows 3–18: Rep Rows 1 and 2 eight more times—48 sts. Work even in St st for 30 more rows—piece measures about 7 (7½, 8)" (18 [19, 20.5] cm) from pick-up row. BO all sts.

Right Pocket Lining

With larger 16" (40-cm) cir and RS facing, beg at lower edge of right pocket opening pick up by knitting 30 sts along the back edge of pocket slit.

Row 1: (WS) Purl to last st, inc 1, p1—1 st inc'd at lower edge of pocket.

Row 2: K2, inc 1, knit to end—1 st inc'd at lower edge of pocket.

Rows 3–18: Rep Rows 1 and 2 eight more times—48 sts. Work even in St st for 30 more rows—piece measures same as left pocket from pick-up row. BO all sts.

Lightly steam (block) fronts and pocket linings, and tack edges of each lining down on inside of front.

Pocket Bands

With larger 16" (40-cm) cir and RS facing, pick up by knitting 24 sts along front edge of pocket opening. Work in K1, P1 Rib for 6 rows. BO in patt. Work second pocket band in the same manner. Tack down selvedges of each pocket band.

Sew buttons into place to correspond to buttonholes.

Inish uses only two cable patterns combined in a simple sequence. No doubt you'll soon be knitting like the Aran knitters of old, following the pattern by looking at your knitting and not at the charts. The jacket is sized like traditional Aran sweaters, by altering the number of stitches in the seed-stitch panels, so the cable design is not disturbed.

Inish

"The work praises the man."

—Irish proverb

FINISHED SIZE

40 (44, 48)" (101.5 [112, 122] cm) chest circumference. Jacket shown measures 40" (101.5 cm). Inish is standard fitting (see fit guidelines on page 136).

YARN 🔢

Shown here: Harrisville New England Knitter's Highland (100% wool; about 200 yd [183 m]/100 g): #28 Iris, 8 (8, 9) skeins.

NEEDLES

Body and sleeves—size 7 (4.5 mm) 24" and 16" (60- and 40-cm) circular needles (cir). Lower edging and front border—size 5 (3.75 mm) 24" (60-cm) cir. Cuffs—size 4 (3.5 mm) set of 4 double-pointed (dpn). Adjust needle size if necessary to obtain the correct gauge.

NOTIONS

Markers (m; several different colors recommended); cable needle (cn); smooth cotton scrap yarn for holders; three ⅜" (1 cm) buttons.

GAUGE

17 stitches and 26 rows = 4" (10 cm) in stockinette using largest needles; 16 stitches and 26 rows = 4" (10 cm) in seed stitch using largest needles; average gauge of charted cable patterns is about 27½ stitches = 4" (10 cm) using largest needles.

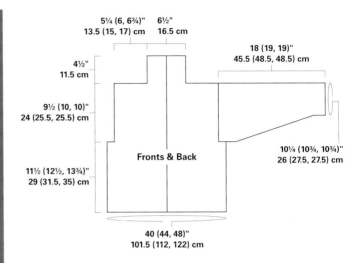

LOWER BODY

With smaller 24" (60-cm) cir, CO 254 (270, 286) sts. Work in seed st for 1 row. **Tip:** To help keep track of the different cable patterns, use different colored markers to indicate each cable panel, i.e., red for 1, blue for 2, green for 3, and so on. **Next row:** (WS) Working Set-up Row for each chart, work 26 sts Chart 1, pm, work 27 sts Chart 2, pm, work 6 (10, 14) seed sts, pm, work 14 sts Chart 3, pm, work 6 (10, 14) seed sts, work 27 sts Chart 2, pm, work 42 sts Chart 4 (working 8-st patt rep box 3 times), pm, work 27 sts Chart 2, pm, work 6 (10, 14) seed sts, pm, work 14 sts Chart 3, pm, work 6 (10, 14) seed sts, pm, work 27 sts Chart 2, pm, work 26 sts Chart 1. Working seed st panels as established, work Rows 1 and 2 of charts. Change to larger 24" (60-cm) cir. Continue in established patts (do not repeat the Set-up Rows), until piece measures 11½ (12½, 13¾)" (29 [31.5, 35] cm) from CO, ending with a RS row.

Reserve Underarms and Fronts

Next Row (WS): Work 74 (79, 84) sts in patt to 1 (2, 3) st(s) after the first Chart 3 cable, place the last 16 (18, 20) sts worked (including m) on holder for left armhole, work 122 (130, 138) sts in patt to 1 (2, 3) st(s) after the second Chart 3 cable, place the last 16 (18, 20) sts worked (including m) on holder for right armhole, work in patt to end of row—58 (61, 64) sts each for right and left front; 106 (112, 118) sts for back. Break yarn. Place both fronts on holders.

BACK

Rejoin yarn to 106 (112, 118) back sts with RS facing. Continue in established patts until piece measures 9 (9½, 9½)" (23 [24, 24] cm) above the underarm, ending with a RS row.

Back Neck and Shoulder Shaping

Next row: (WS) Work 32 (35, 38) sts in patt for back left shoulder, place rem 74 (77, 80) sts on holder. Continue in established patt for 4 more rows—piece measures about 9½ (10, 10)" (24 [25.5, 25.5] cm) above underarm. Break yarn, and place left shoulder sts on holder. Place 74 (77, 81) sts held sts on needle and rejoin yarn with WS facing. BO center 42 sts, work 32 (35, 38) sts in patt to end for right back shoulder. Continue in established patt for 4 more rows—piece measures same as right shoulder above underarm. Break yarn and place right shoulder sts on holder.

LEFT FRONT

Place 58 (61, 64) held left front sts on larger cir and rejoin yarn with RS facing at armhole edge. Continue in established patts until piece measures 9½ (10, 10)" (24 [25.5, 25.5] cm) above the underarm, ending with a WS row. With RS facing, place first 32 (35, 38) sts on holder for left front shoulder, then place rem 26 sts on separate holder for left collar. Make a note of the last patt row completed so you can resume working the collar with the correct row.

RIGHT FRONT

Place 58 (61, 64) held right front sts on larger cir and rejoin yarn with RS facing at neck edge. Continue in established patts until piece measures 9½ (10, 10)" (24 [25.5, 25.5] cm) above the underarm, ending with a WS row. With RS facing, place first 26 sts on holder for right collar, then place rem 32 (35, 38) sts on holder for left front shoulder. As for left front, make a note of the last patt row completed.

JOIN SHOULDERS

With RS of pieces touching and WS facing outward, join 32 (35, 38) front and back shoulder sts using the three-needle bind-off method.

SLEEVES

Notes: Sleeves are worked in the round from cuffs upward, then attached to the body by binding off the live sleeve sts tog with stitches picked up around the armhole opening using the three-needle bind-off method. The cable panel from Chart 5 is centered on the sleeve, and new stitches at each side are worked in seed stitch. Because the sleeve is knit in the round, read all chart rows from right to left as RS rounds.

Chart 1

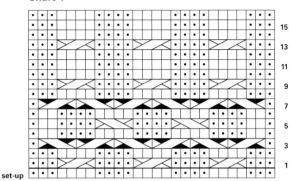

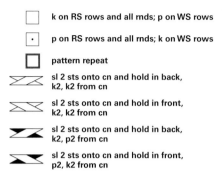

- ☐ k on RS rows and all rnds; p on WS rows
- · p on RS rows and all rnds; k on WS rows
- ☐ pattern repeat
- sl 2 sts onto cn and hold in back, k2, k2 from cn
- sl 2 sts onto cn and hold in front, k2, k2 from cn
- sl 2 sts onto cn and hold in back, k2, p2 from cn
- sl 2 sts onto cn and hold in front, p2, k2 from cn

Chart 2

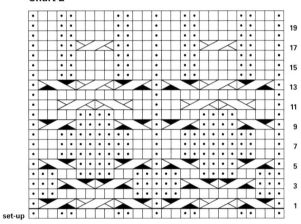

Chart 3

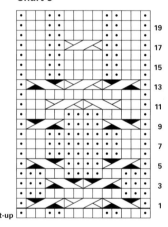

Cuff

With dpn in smallest size, CO 56 (58, 58) sts. Join for working in the rnd, and pm for beg of rnd. Work in seed st for 10 rnds, inc 9 sts evenly spaced in last rnd—65 (67, 67) sts. **Next rnd:** K1, work 3 (4, 4) seed sts, pm, work Rnd 1 of Chart 5 over 58 sts (working 8-st patt rep box 5 times), pm, work 3, (4, 4) seed sts. Change to 16" (40-cm) cir in largest size. **Note:** Work the first st of every rnd as k1; shaping increases will be worked on each side of this knit st. Keeping first st of rnd as k1, work 5 more rnds in established patt. **Inc rnd:** Using the backward-loop method

for all incs, k1, inc 1, work in patt to end, inc 1—2 sts inc'd. Continuing in established patt, rep the inc rnd every 6th rnd 14 (15, 16) times, working new sts into seed st—95 (99, 101) sts. Continue in established patt until piece measures 18 (19, 19)" (45.5 [48.5, 48.5] cm) from CO. Place sts on holder, or leave on needle if attaching to body immediately.

Set up Armholes and Attach Sleeves

Note: Leave underarm holder strings in place until after the underarm sts have been attached, then remove holders.

Chart 4

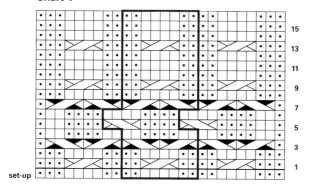

set-up

Chart 5

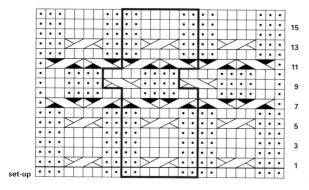

set-up

With 24" (60-cm) cir in largest size and RS facing, beg in center of 14-st Chart 3 cable, work 8 (9, 10) sts from holder as k2tog 4 (4, 5) times, k0 (1, 0), pick up by knitting 43 (44, 45) sts along armhole edge to shoulder, 1 st in shoulder join, then 43 (44, 45) sts down to underarm, work rem 8 (9, 10) sts from holder as k0 (1, 0), k2tog 4 (4, 5) times—95 (99, 101) sts. With RS of pieces touching and WS facing outward, beg in center of underarm, join 95 (99, 101) live sts at top of sleeve to 95 (99, 101) sts picked up around armhole using the three-needle bind-off method.

FINISHING

Collar

Place 26 held left front sts on 16" (40-cm) cir in largest size, and rejoin yarn with RS facing. Continuing in established patt from Chart 1, work 30 rows in patt. Bind off. Place 26 held right front sts on 16" (40-cm) cir in largest size. Work 30 rows in patt as for left collar. Bind off. Sew selvedges of collar extensions along back neck edge so that bound off edges meet exactly at center back, easing to fit as necessary. Sew collar tog at center back neck.

Front Border

With smaller 24" (60-cm) needle and RS facing, beg at lower edge of right front pick up by knitting 90 (95, 100) sts along right front to the center back collar join, then 90 (95, 100) sts along left front to lower edge of left front—180 (190, 200) sts. Knit 4 rows, ending with a RS row. BO on next WS row as if to knit.

Buttonholes and Buttons

These are already built in! The cable crossing in Row 3 of Chart 1 creates a wonderful, perfect-size hole in the center of the first cable-enclosed diamond at the right front edge of the jacket. Go ahead, put your finger in there and find it. Because every diamond along the edge has one, these buttonholes are perfectly spaced, beautifully incorporated into the design, and totally invisible when not in use. It's easy to place the buttons as well. Sew a button into the center of each corresponding diamond on the left front. You can decide how many buttons to put on; the jacket shown here uses 3 buttons. Sew buttons in position to correspond to your chosen buttonholes.

Materials &
Techniques

Successful projects depend on the choice
of appropriate materials and techniques.
The knitter has many options when it comes to
yarn, and the knitting literature abounds with
techniques for using it. In this chapter you'll
find the information necessary to create the
jackets in this book.

MATERIALS

Buttons

Love those buttons! The right button can really make a jacket. Buttons, whether "working" or used as embellishment with another type of closure, give you an opportunity to put a "signature" on your jackets. Have fun choosing your buttons. Unless you are positive that the buttons you have chosen for your jacket are washable, sew them on after washing and blocking the garment. Special button pins, available in most fabric stores, will work to temporarily attach buttons that you do not want to wash.

Stitch Holders

Try using contrasting-color, smooth and lightweight cotton yarn or string to hold stitches. On circular garments in particular, the stitching and cutting is much easier if the stitches aren't all bunched up on rigid metal holders. Use a yarn needle threaded with scrap yarn and slip the stitches to be held purlwise onto the yarn. Be generous and give yourself lots of yarn for each holder. Tie the scrap yarn so the stitches can't slip off. When picking up the stitches from the holder, leave the holder in until you are sure that all the stitches are on the needle and you are happily knitting along again.

Substituting Yarns

So many yarns, so little time! The sources for the yarns used in this book are listed on page 143. If you decide to try a different yarn than what is called for in the patterns, you can do so successfully by following these guidelines.

1. Choose a yarn with the same gauge as the yarn used in the pattern; a different weight yarn will have a different stitch gauge, and your jacket will have a dramatically different look and fit. The Craft Yarn Council of America's Standard Yarn Weight System symbols have been included with each pattern to assist you in making an appropriate yarn choice.

ABBREVIATIONS

beg	begin(s); beginning
BO	bind off
CC	contrast color
cir	circular
cn	cable needle
cm	centimeter(s)
CO	cast on
dec	decrease(s), decreasing
dpn	double-pointed needles
foll	follow(s), following
g	grams
inc	increase(s), increasing
inc 1	increase 1 stitch by a adding backward loop
k	knit
k2tog	knit 2 stitches together
k1f&b	knit in the front and the back of the stitch (an increase)
kwise	as if to knit
m	marker
MC	main color
mm	millimeter
p	purl
patt(s)	pattern(s)
pm	place marker
psso	pass slipped st over
p2sso	pass 2 slipped sts over
pwise	as if to purl
rem	remain(s); remaining
rnd	round
RS	right side
Sl	slip stitch. Unless specified otherwise, slip purlwise
Ssk	slip 2 stitches individually to right needle knitwise, slip left needle through front of stitches, and k2tog through back loops
st(s)	stitch(es)
St st	stockinette stitch
tog	together
WS	wrong side
wyf	with yarn in front
wyb	with yarn in back
yo	yarn over needle

Symbol	Stitches in 4" of Stockinette St	Recommended Needle Size
0 LACE	33–40	000–1 (1.5–2.25 mm)
1 SUPER FINE	27–32	1–3 (2.25–3.25 mm)
2 FINE	23–26	3–5 (3.25–3.75 mm)
3 LIGHT	21–24	5–7 (3.75–4.5 mm)
4 MEDIUM	16–20	7–9 (4.5–5.5 mm)
5 BULKY	12–15	9–11 (5.5–8 mm)
6 SUPER BULKY	6–11	11 and larger (8 mm and larger)

2. Buy the amount of yardage specified in the pattern. Your local yarn shop can be most helpful here as they have resources that list the weight and yardage of hundreds of yarns and can make sure that you get enough of your substitute yarn to finish the project. The ball bands of most yarns provide this information as well. To determine the yardage you need, multiply the number of yards per ball for the original yarn by the number of balls required. Then divide this sum by the yards per ball for the substitute yarn; the result will be the number of balls you need of the substitute yarn.

3. If the yarn you have purchased has a different color, fiber content and/or texture, please do a swatch before deciding to use the yarn; it may not behave or look the way you would expect just from seeing it in the ball.

TECHNIQUES
Backward-loop Cast-on
Twist the yarn into a loop and place the loop on the right needle. Repeat for desired number of stitches.

Crochet Chain
Begin with a slipknot or stitch on the hook. Yarn over hook and pull loop through. Repeat for required number of stitches.

Crochet Slip Stitch
Insert hook into existing stitch from front to back. Yarn over hook and pull loop through.

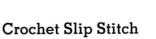

Decreases
Ssk	Slip two stitches individually to right needle knitwise, slip left needle through front of stitches and knit them together through back loops.
K2tog	Knit two stitches together.

Fit Guidelines
The Craft Yarn Council of America's Standard Fitting Guidelines have been included with each pattern to illustrate the amount of ease the jacket is meant to incorporate. Measure the chest you are knitting for, then use this chart to determine the right size to knit.

Jacket Fit Chart

FIT	AMOUNT OF EASE
Close-fitting	1–2" (2.5–5 cm)
Standard-fitting	2–4" (5–10 cm)
Loose-fitting	4–6" (10–15 cm)
Oversize	6" (15 cm) or more

Gauge

Gauge means how many stitches and rows there are per inch in a chosen yarn and pattern. Changing the needle size alters this gauge—using a smaller needle results in more stitches and rows per inch, while using a larger needle results in fewer stitches and rows per inch. Always do a swatch to make sure you get the right gauge for your chosen size.

Some of the jackets are sized by changing the number of stitches and some are sized by altering the stitch gauge. The sizing method was determined by the jacket's design. Sizing by altering the gauge maintains one set number of stitches that applies to all sizes, thus keeping the integrity of the pattern and ensuring that the knitter gets the garment shown in the photo. Regardless of the sizing method used, getting the proper gauge gives a mathematical certainty to your sizing while preventing disruption of a carefully planned design. Please do a swatch and be sure your gauge is correct (see Swatching, page 138).

Gauges for the jackets have been given in stockinette stitch where practical and in pattern stitch where the stitch is simple (box stitch, garter stitch) or it is beneficial to try out the stitch technique before proceeding (slip stitch). Two-color projects require two-color swatches to measure the gauge and those detailed instructions are given on page 140 (see two-color knitting techniques). For those patterns with cables or intricate single-color stitch patterns, a stockinette-stitch gauge has been provided to make your knitting life more pleasant. In these cases the stockinette-stitch swatch has been knitted with the same needle size as the jacket pattern stitch. Achieve the stockinette-stitch gauge and then use that same size needle for the pattern stitch. In this manner the correct gauge for even very complicated cable patterns can be achieved by doing just a stockinette-stitch swatch. Of course trying out the stitch pattern is always a good idea, and if you feel the need to do so, follow your instincts!

Increases

Backward Loop	Twist the yarn into a loop and place it on the right needle. Tighten until snug.
K1f&b	Knit into the front of the stitch, leave it on the needle, then knit into the back of the stitch (two stitches made in one) and slip off.

Pick Up by Knitting

Holding the garment with right side facing you, insert a needle from front to back, one stitch in from the edge. Wrap the yarn around the needle as if to knit and pull the yarn through, forming a stitch on the needle. Repeat this procedure until the required number of stitches are on the needle.

Provisional Cast-on

There are many ways to cast on provisionally. The crochet-over-the-needle method is easy to start, stitches are easy to count, and, when done with a smooth scrap yarn, it comes out quickly.

With contrasting smooth cotton scrap yarn, make a slipknot and place it on a crochet hook. Hold the yarn in your left hand and the hook in your right. Hold a needle on top of the long strand of yarn in your left hand. *With hook, draw a loop over the needle and through the slipknot **(Figure 1)**. You will now have pulled the yarn over the knitting needle and cast on a stitch. Place the yarn behind the knitting needle **(Figure 2)** and repeat from * until you have the required number of stitches on the needle. With the last loop still on the crochet hook, cut the yarn and slip the tail through the loop on the hook. Pull up loosely. When you're ready to take out the cast-on, pull the tail out of the last loop and tug on it to unchain the cast-on edge and place the stitches on a needle.

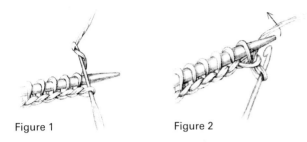

Figure 1

Figure 2

Short Rows *(Wrap and Turn)*

Knit to the specified point and leave the yarn where it is. *Slip the next stitch as if to purl **(Figure 1)**. Bring yarn to the front (to the back on a purl row) and slip the stitch back to the left needle **(Figure 2)**—you have just wrapped the stitch. Turn. Bring the yarn into the proper position for the next stitch and continue as directed **(Figure 3)**.

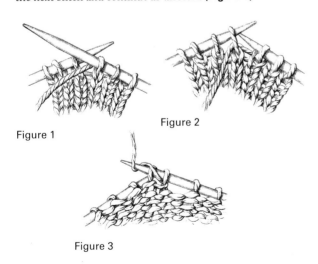

Figure 1

Figure 2

Figure 3

Swatching

Swatching is the most important thing that you can do to make sure your garment both looks and fits the way you expect it to. The time you take to knit a swatch will be well spent. By swatching you not only assure that you will get a garment that fits its intended body, but you can also decide if you like the yarn and the pattern and how the fabric will behave when steamed or washed. Your swatch is your best friend! Keep swatching until you get it right.

It's easy to make a swatch. Cast on at least thirty stitches and work in the stitch pattern specified for the gauge in the pattern. Steam or wash your swatch and allow it to dry. Measure the entire width of the swatch and divide the width into the number of stitches that you have cast on. The resulting number is the number of stitches you are getting per inch. If the pattern states that you need a gauge of twenty-eight stitches to four inches, you need to be getting seven stitches to the inch (twenty-eight stitches divided by four inches). Where possible the patterns in this book require only a stockinette-stitch or garter-stitch swatch; the two-color patterns will need to be swatched using the two-color stranding method. Read the section on two-color knitting techniques for detailed two-color swatch instructions. If the gauge is given in pattern stitch, it is because it is basically a simple pattern stitch or it is a good idea to practice this technique before beginning.

Three-needle Bind-off

Place the two sets of stitches to be joined on separate needles. With the right sides * together, hold the needles parallel in your left hand. With a third needle in your right hand, join the yarn and knit together one stitch from each needle (one from the front needle, one from the back needle). Repeat this on the next pair of stitches. You will now have two stitches on the right-hand needle. Pass the first stitch on the right needle over the second stitch as in regular bind off. Repeat the procedure, knitting front and back stitches together and then binding off until all the stitches are bound off. *If you want a ridge on the outside, hold wrong sides together.

Three-needle Bind-off to Attach Sleeves to Body

Place sleeve stitches on a circular needle. With a second circular needle and beginning at the center of the underarm, pick up stitches around the armhole (the same number of stitches as there are at the top of the sleeve). Matching the center of the underarm with the first stitch of the sleeve, make sure the correct sides of the sleeve and the body are together as called for in the pattern: right sides together will produce a smooth seam and wrong sides together will produce a ridge on the outside where the body and sleeve meet. Using a third needle, bind the armhole and sleeve stitches off together as for the three-needle bind-off described above.

Blocking and Handwashing Guide

Blocking is the penultimate finishing tool. Blocking smoothes patterns, straightens seams, and gives your garments a professional look. I always block when the jacket is wet, after handwashing (see below). In addition, a light steaming before finishing and washing "sets" the stitches, especially in two-color patterns, and adds to the smoothness of the finished fabric. A steamed piece is often easier to work with when picking up stitches or finishing.

To steam, lay the jacket out on a flat surface and place a definitely damp pressing cloth on top. With an iron on steam setting, lightly graze the pressing cloth—you should hear a pleasing hiss of steam—apply no real pressure to the jacket. Remove the pressing cloth and carefully smooth the warm fabric lightly with your hands. Steam the fabric and the seams and let the jacket cool. Then it's off to handwashing for the final blocking.

If you have doubts about washing a particular article, first wash a swatch as a test. Fill a large sink with warm (body temperature) water. Very cold or very hot water "shocks" the fibers, so avoid extremes. Use a mild soap or your favorite product. I like to use liquid castile soap. Use one or two teaspoons of soap and mix into water with your hand.

Place article to be washed in the water. Gently push it down and squeeze to get it thoroughly wet. Let it soak for ten minutes. Squeeze soapy water through the fabric a few times. Let the water drain out of the sink, pushing the article against the sink to remove most of the soapy water. Refill the sink with cool water. Gently knead article to rinse out soap. Drain sink again and repeat rinse procedure. If a dye is bleeding excessively, simply continue rinsing until the rinse water is clear. You may add a teaspoon of vinegar to the last rinse to help "set" the dye.

After the last rinse, allow the article to drain well in sink, pushing it against the sides of sink to remove most of the water. Do not wring. Roll the article in a large towel and squeeze so the towel soaks up the excess water or run the article through a washing machine spin cycle. Place the article in the machine and set the cycle selector to a slow spin cycle. Allow machine to spin for two or three minutes and then remove the article and lay it out to dry. A machine-spun article will dry more quickly than a towel-rolled one. If stretching is a concern, as with some cottons, put the article inside a pillowcase before spinning.

Lay out article on a blocking board or on a large towel on the floor and gently smooth out with your hands. Use a tape measure to check the finished measurements. Pin into place if necessary with rustproof pins. Let dry completely.

Chart Reading

Each square on the chart represents a stitch. The legend for the chart will indicate which symbols stand for which colors and/or stitches. Charts are read from bottom to top. When knitting back and forth, right-side rows are read from right to left and wrong-side rows from left to right. When knitting circularly, all rounds are read from right to left.

Lace charts show right-side rows only. When working a lace chart back and forth, purl all wrong-side rows. When working a lace chart circularly, knit one row between each one shown on the chart.

Enlarge charts on a copying machine, if necessary, to make them easier to read. A magnetic board will help you keep track of charted patterns. Put the chart on the board and place the magnetic strip directly above the row being worked. Move the magnet up as each row is completed. Sticky notes work, too, and can be used to keep pattern notes as well.

Two-color Knitting Techniques
Swatching

When knitting your swatch, start with the suggested needle for your chosen size and change the needle as necessary to obtain the given gauge for your size garment. To get an accurate gauge measurement for circular two-color knitting, make your swatch as follows. **Note:** When working with two colors in a row, knit the first and last stitches with both colors held together to anchor the yarns and produce an even tension.

With one color of yarn and circular needle, cast on thirty-two stitches (thirty pattern stitches plus two anchor stitches). Knit one row. At the end of the row, break off the yarn leaving a three-inch tail. Do not turn work. Instead, slide all the stitches to the other end of the needle, join both colors, leaving a three-inch tail, and knit the second row (one anchor stitch with both colors held together, thirty stitches from chart using two-color stranding, and one more anchor stitch with both colors held together). Break yarns, leaving a three-inch tail. Repeat this knitting and sliding, breaking and rejoining the yarns on every row. In this way you are knitting every row (no purling) and simulating the gauge that you will have when you are knitting every row on your circular project.

You may tie the ends of the yarn together on the sides

to keep the proper tension. Tie the ends as you knit or wait until the swatch is finished but tie them before washing and measuring. Block your swatch (see Blocking and Handwashing Guide, page 139). When it is dry, measure its entire width between the edge stitches, i.e., do not count the two outside stitches.

Stranding and Catching

When knitting with two colors in each row, carry the yarn not in use loosely across the back of the work. When you are finished with one color, drop it and begin knitting with the other color. To keep the yarns from twisting when carrying them across each other, bring one strand underneath the other and bring the other strand over the top. Make a note of which color goes over and which goes under and be consistent throughout the garment.

To avoid leaving long carried threads that may catch on buttons or fingers, don't carry the yarn not in use over more than an inch's worth of stitches. If the pattern requires that the yarn be carried over more than an inch, catch it in back at least once, more than once for very long strands. To catch the yarn, simply twist it around the knitting yarn so that it is held in place by the next knitted stitch. The carried yarn will not show through to the front when it is twisted around the knitting yarn correctly. If it is necessary to catch the carried yarn on several consecutive rounds, do not catch it at the same place—knit one more or one less stitch before twisting the yarns. Carried yarns caught on the same stitch on consecutive rows will show through to the front between the knitted stitches.

Tension in Two-color Knitting

Always maintain a relaxed tension while stranding and catching the yarn being carried. If the yarn is pulled too tightly across the back of the work, the knitting will draw up and look puckered. To keep the carried yarn at a good tension, spread the stitches on the right needle out on the needle before bringing the carried yarn across the back. This will allow for plenty of slack in the carried yarn and keep the knitted fabric smooth.

Steeks

There are several methods of preparing and securing a steek; this is one of them. While the knitter is free to explore other methods, keep in mind that there may be adjustments required in the set up of the steek and in the pattern if an alternate steeking method is used.

A steek consists of a number of extra stitches that will be cut to create an opening in a circularly knitted garment. To make a steek, first put stitches on hold as called for in the pattern. On the right-hand needle, cast on the required number of stitches (with both strands held together if knitting with two colors) using the backward-loop method (see page 136) or any cast on, then continue knitting in the round. Place markers on each side of the steek so that you recognize it when you come to it.

When working with two colors in a row, alternate the colors in the steek on every stitch and every row to be sure that each color is secure before cutting.

Shaping Around a Steek

Whether for neckline or for armholes, openings are shaped by working decreases on each side of the steek stitches. Make mirror-image decreases by using k2tog on one side and ssk on the other. Keep a plain knit stitch on each side between the decrease and the steek; the decreases will not fall awkwardly on the very edge of the opening and the plain knit stitch will provide a clean edge from which to later pick up stitches.

Stitching and Cutting

After the body of the jacket is complete, the steeks are stitched on a sewing machine and cut to make the openings. First securely work in the ends of yarn along the edge of the steek. Be sure to close any gap that occurs between the steek and the first stitch of the row. Mark the center stitch of the steek by basting with yarn of a highly contrasting color. Make sure that most of the basting thread shows on the front so you can use it as your stitching guide. Set your sewing machine for a short stitch. Make two rows of machine stitching on each side of the center stitch. As you are stitching, make sure the knitted fabric does not pucker—stretch the fabric vertically slightly.

After completing all four rows of machine stitching, cut the knitted fabric on the basting line down the center of the steek, between the rows of machine stitching.

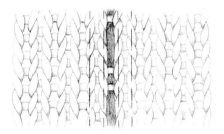

Stitch Patterns

Garter Stitch When working back and forth, knit every row. When working circularly, alternately knit a round and purl a round.

Stockinette Stitch When working back and forth, knit the right-side rows and purl the wrong-side rows. When working circularly, knit every round.

Slip Stitch Unless otherwise specified, always slip the stitches as if to purl, regardless of whether the yarn is to be held in front or in back of the work.

Acknowledgments

No one can whistle a symphony. It takes an orchestra to play it.

—Prof. H.E. Luccock, Yale University

To my wonderful test knitters and angels, Anne Reed, Lynn Gates, Carmen Hall, Shaaron Jacobs, Linda Lutz, and Joann Arndt, thank you for sharing your talents and patience and for making sure that what came off my needles made sense on paper.

To Judith Durant, editor extraordinaire, all my gratitude for your grace, your creativity, and your friendship. And to Lori Gayle, technical editor, thanks for applying your skillful insight and expertise. We all need great editors!

My appreciation goes to the editorial staff at Interweave, Rebecca Campbell and Tricia Wadell in particular, who allowed this book to become what it was meant to be, and to the production staff whose talents have brought it from possibility to reality.

Many thanks to Joe Coca for the outstanding photography in *Knitted Jackets* and to Timothy Miles Basgall for the author's photo that is on the Interweave website. Thanks also to Northern Colorado Feeders Supply, Patty Spencer, the Northern Hotel, the Armstrong Hotel, and Steve and Missy Levinger for their assistance with the photography.

To Linda Ligon and Marilyn Murphy, thank you for Interweave. The knitting world is much richer for its influence.

My great gratitude goes to Meg Swansen and Schoolhouse Press, La Lana Wools, Weaving Southwest, Harrisville Designs, Brown Sheep Company, Knitting Fever, and Philosopher's Wool for generously supplying yarns for *Knitted Jackets*.

I have deepest appreciation and respect for all the knitters in my life who continue to inspire and encourage this passion for knitting. All my thanks, always.

And to Gary Oberle, my husband and dearest friend, thanks again for your beautiful linocuts, for sharing your artist's heart, and for knowing that together we could do this again.

Resources

Yarn

Berroco Inc.
PO Box 367
14 Elmdale Rd.
Uxbridge, MA 01569-0367
berroco.com

Brown Sheep Company Inc.
100662 County Road 16
Mitchell, NE 69357
(800) 826-9136
brownsheep.com

Cascade Yarns Inc.
PO Box 58168
Tukwila, WA 98138
(800) 548-1048
cascadeyarns.com

Cheryl Oberle Designs
3315 Newton St.
Denver, CO 80211
(303) 433-9205
cheryloberle.com

Diakeito
www.diakeito.co.jp

Harrisville Designs Inc.
41 Main St.
Harrisville, NH 03450
(603) 827-3333
harrisville.com

Henry's Attic
5 Mercury Ave.
Monroe, NY 10950-3736
(845) 783-3930

Jo Sharp Hand Knitting Yarns
PO Box 357
Albany, WA 96331
josharp.com

Knitting Fever/KFI
PO Box 336
315 Bayview Ave.
Amityville, NY 11701
(516) 546-3600
knittingfever.com

La Lana Wools
136-C Paseo del Pueblo Norte
Taos, NM 87571
(575) 758-9631
(888) 377-9631
lalanawools.com

Philosopher's Wool Company
Inverhuron, ON
Canada N0G 2T0
(519) 368-5354
philosopherswool.com

Schoolhouse Press
6899 Cary Bluff
Pittsville, WI 54466
(800) 968-5648
schoolhousepress.com

Skacel Collection Inc.
PO Box 88110
Seattle, WA 98138-2110
(800) 255-1278
skacelknitting.com

Weaving Southwest
216 B Paseo del Pueblo Norte
Taos, NM 87571
(505) 758-0433
(800) 765-1272
weavingsouthwest.com

Shawl Pins

Cats and Cobswebs
Rose Marie Diem
PO Box 1555
Duarte, CA 91009-4555
(626) 303-0543
artsights.com/cobwebs/

Designs by Romi
Rosemary Hill
73 Bosworth Ln.
Geyserville, CA 95441
(707) 857-3399
designsbyromi.com

Creative Designs Unlimited
Stephen and Damaris Hanson
274 Vienna St.
San Francisco, CA 94112
(415) 334-1414
shawlpins.com

Bibliography

Forster, E.M. *Howards End.* New York: Signet, 1992.

Gibson-Roberts, Priscilla A. *Salish Indian Sweaters: A Pacific Northwest Tradition.* Saint Paul, Minnesota: Dos Tejedoras, 1989.

Hiatt, June Hemmons. *The Principles of Knitting.* New York: Simon and Schuster, 1988.

Hibi, Sadao. *The Colors of Japan.* Tokyo: Kodansha International, 2002.

Kempner, Beryl, ed. *The Harmony Guide to Aran Knitting.* London: Lyric Books Limited, 1991.

Koren, Leonard. *Wabi-Sabi for Artists, Designers, Poets & Philosophers.* Berkeley, California: Stone Bridge Press, 1994.

McGregor, Sheila. *The Complete Book of Traditional Scandinavian Knitting.* New York: St. Martin's Press, 1984.

Tilke, Max. *Costume Patterns and Designs.* New York: Rizzoli International Publications, 1990.

Vanberg, Bent, and Karin Hybbestad Schwantes. *Norwegian Bunads.* Oslo: Hjemmenes Forlag, 1991.

Walker, Barbara G. *Charted Knitting Designs: A Treasury of Knitting Patterns.* New York: Charles Scribner's Sons, 1968.

—*Charted Knitting Designs: A Third Treasury of Knitting Patterns.* New York: Charles Scribner's Sons, 1972.

Zimmerman, Elizabeth. *Knitting without Tears.* New York: Charles Scribner's Sons, 1971.

Index

abbreviations 135

backward-loop increase 137
backward-loop cast-on 136
bind-off 138–139
blocking 139
buttons 135

cast-on 136, 137
charts, reading 139–140
color stranding 140
color knitting techniques, two- 140–141
Craft Yarn Council of America yarn chart 135
Craft Yarn Council of America fitting guidelines 136–137
crochet chain 136
crochet slip stitch 136

cutting steeks 141

decreases 136

garter stitch 141
gauge 137

increases 137

k1f&b increase 137
k2tog decrease 136

pick up by knitting 137
provisional cast-on 137–138

shaping around steeks 141
short rows 138
slip stitch 141

ssk decrease 136
steeks 141
stitch holders 135
stitching steeks 141
stitch patterns 141
stockinette stitch 141
stranding 140
swatches 138, 140

tension in two-color knitting 140–141
three-needle bind-off 138–139

washing 139

yarns, catching color 140
yarns, substituting 135–136
yarn weight standards chart 136